Project Management Institute

THINGS YOUR PMO IS DOING WRONG

by Michael Hatfield

ISBN: 978-1-933890-55-5

Published by: Project Management Institute, Inc.
                         14 Campus Blvd.
                         Newtown Square, Pennsylvania 19073-3299 USA.
                         Phone: +610-356-4600
                         Fax: +610-356-4647
                         E-mail: customercare@pmi.org
                         Internet: www.pmi.org

To inquire about discounts for resale or educational purposes, please contact the PMI Book Service Center.
                         PMI Book Service Center
                         P.O. Box 932683, Atlanta, GA 31193-2683 USA
                         Phone: 1-866-276-4764 (within the U.S. or Canada) or
                         +1-770-280-4129 (globally)
                         Fax: +1-770-280-4113
                         E-mail: book.orders@pmi.org

Acknowledgements

I didn't write this book. Well, actually, I did write it, but there's no way the ideas in here are exclusively mine. Besides the properly attributed references, the ideas in this book have been vetted and evaluated by some of the most advanced minds in the field of project management. Here's a partial list, placed in alphabetical order so that I don't have to evaluate who was more important among a field of outstanding management minds:

Joseph Baehr
Bud Baker
Ted Ball
John Benner
Armando Cordova
Howard Daudistel
Kurt Deshayes
Donny Ellsworth
Kathleen Fillmore
Gary Fillmore
Mark Forrey
Dan Goldfischer
Mike Grijalva
David Hampton
Lisa Hampton
Greg Hanson

Rhonda Hanson
Anderson Hatfield
Leroy Hatfield
Gary Humphries
Sandy Jenkins
Walt Kirchner
Brett Kniss
Toby Lovato
Chris Madigan
Doug Marbourg
Dave Maurer
Randy Mendenhall
Larry Murphy
Katherine Nelson
Jim Noel

Lewis Peach
David Post
Stan Prueitt
Alice Skehan
Jim Sloan
Jeff Sorroche
Patrice Stevens
Terry Sutton
Fred Tarantino
Antonio Tavares
Steve Treibel
Robert Turner
Roger Weinke
Ray Wood
Lance "Woody" Woodworth

I'm probably forgetting some names, and I'm not at all claiming that these people will necessarily agree with the assertions and conclusions in this book. However, I do owe them a debt of gratitude, and I wanted them to know it.

I also need to thank Professor William C. Dowling, currently of Rutgers University but formerly of the University of New Mexico, for teaching me how to write, which was no small feat. Indeed, any effective turn of a phrase included in this book is due to his excellent tutelage, and any mistake in syntax is due to my not paying enough attention in his classes. I thank Marcia Daudistel, Barbara Walsh, and Donn Greenberg for teaching me how to prepare a manuscript for publishing.

Finally, I want to thank Mary Kay Anderson, and Troy Hatfield for putting up with me while I committed to keyboard my thoughts on why project management offices so often fail and what can be done about it.

What this Book is About, and How It's Different from Others on the Subject

I wrote this book because every other tome I've encountered on the subject of implementing project management or advancing its capability always came across like it was scolding its readers. Standards say organizations "must do this" and "must do that" to "make" themselves successful. Must. Make. Kind of makes me wonder, what if they don't? Will the authors of these standards come and lean on the recalcitrant members of your organization, reminiscent of the "*Nobody* expects the Spanish Inquisition!" skit from Monty Python?

Other advisors on the subject of advancing project management capabilities resort to what I call "eat-your-peas-style" hectoring (or letting you know what is good for you, much as a parent would a child). Contrast the tone of project management standards with this quote from one of the most successful practitioners of project management techniques in the world, the irreplaceable Randy Mendenhall: "That's stupid. We ain't doin' it that way."

As these two references represent the conventional wisdom in the field of program and portfolio management, they illustrate perfectly the conundrum facing project management office (PMO) personnel (or anyone who wants their organization to perform project management techniques): Is there any way of doing this, rather than begging or threatening? The short answer is, yes, there are ways of successfully advancing project management and the PMO's agenda. But the path ahead is fraught with dangers, forks in the road that lead nowhere, mirages, and, yes, enemies. Your ability to adopt the best technical approach and avoid the pitfalls that have ruined so many other attempts is the only thing that can possibly deliver success. This book is about which technical approach is best and how to avoid related dangers.

Another difficult aspect about the writings on this subject is a certain degree of muddleheadedness, or fuzzy logic that has crept in to almost all management writing. I found this gem in *Organizational Behavior and Performance*, (Szilagyi and Wallace 1987, page 229):

> "Situational factors influencing intragroup behavior include group size, social density, task, and group composition. Research has shown that, under certain conditions, each factor can affect group performance. The most important concept for managers to remember from this

discussion is that type of task is a key determinant of the extent to which the other factors influence group performance. Stated simply, the effects of group size and social density on performance and the success of group development depend to a large extent on the task performed by the group."

I think they're trying to say that there's a bunch of different factors that come into play when assessing group performance, but the inclusion of terms such as "social density" fills the room with fog. Surely, the basic point they're making is simply too obvious to make in a graduate-level management text, so it's worded in such a way as to deflect criticism.

A common method for introducing poorly defined concepts as legitimate insights is to represent them in a graphic form, usually with boxes and arrows. These infernal graphics are part flow diagram, part Venn diagram, and almost always stupid. But as any MBA candidate can tell you, if the concept is too vague to be clearly described in words, drawing it out won't help other than to further demonstrate the idea's poor definition.

Unfortunately, writings on management in general and project management in particular have become infested with high-sounding vagaries, delivered with massive doses of arrogance, pretentiousness, and condescension. It is my intent to cut through the muddleheadedness, but in the process I'm going to present ideas that will strike you as counterintuitive. In each case though, I promise to state my case clearly and back it up with succinctly stated reasoning and the evidence I'm considering as part of my argument. In this sense, this book is like no other on the subject of project management implementation, because I'm not writing it with any sense of fear that critics will come along later, tear it to shreds, and then not let me into the project management presenter's clubhouse. I'm so confident that the tactics I discuss in this book will work that when the readers create their own clubhouse of successful PMOs, they'll readily welcome me into their tree house, where we can drink root beer and read comic books until our moms call us home for dinner, leaving the previous project management elite sputtering with rage.

And so, without further adieu, here's what your PMO is doing wrong, and, more importantly, how to do it right.

Table of Contents

PART 1

Tactics that Don't Work

Mr. Praline: He's not pining! He's passed on! This parrot is no more! He has ceased to be! He's expired and gone to meet 'is maker! He's a stiff! Bereft of life, he rests in peace! If you hadn't nailed him to the perch, he'd be pushing up the daisies! His metabolic processes are now history! He's off the twig! He's kicked the bucket; he's shuffled off his mortal coil, run down the curtain, and joined the bleedin' choir invisible!! *THIS IS AN EX-PARROT!!*

—*Monty Python's Flying Circus,* 1969

If you are reading this sentence, then I know something about you: you have gained some level of expertise in the field of project management, have had some success in using its techniques, and perceive that both you and your organization could realize much more such success from advancing project management capability. But there's a problem: not everybody in your organization is willing to do project management. In fact, many of your associates, knowingly or not, are actively working against the widespread use of project management techniques, keeping your odds of being able to properly manage your work frustratingly low. Many projects—perhaps even yours—are in danger of becoming managerial train wrecks, damaging profits and careers, perhaps permanently. You've tried to get your accountants to track costs based on work rather than organization, have pressured your team leaders to fill out work packages and work breakdown structure dictionaries, and sang the praises of critical path scheduling to your superiors, all in vain. Don't they see? Don't they understand that *not* doing project management is tempting disaster?

The good news is that you can implement project management techniques and further project management maturity, and it's easier than your previous attempts' frustrations have led you to believe. The bad news is that the tactics proscribed by conventional wisdom and virtually all of the experts simply don't work, and if you're attempting to use them, you're wasting valuable time and energy in an arena where wasting time and energy is usually fatal to the project management office.

A Few Questions

On his nationally syndicated radio show, Rush Limbaugh once said, "If you want to be successful, find out what people want, and give it to them." In the world of project management, what is it that people want? They want to have their project work delivered on-time, within budget, and done well. How do project managers do this? They do this through their decisions, both strategic and tactical, that impact every dimension of the project. In fact, the macro-organization can be defined as the sum total of the decisions of each of its members, from the decision of the receptionists to greet customers cheerfully, all the way to the decisions of the stockholders to buy or sell. Unfortunately, there is no way to guarantee that every project manager's decision will be the right one. The only way to improve the organization's project management capability is to ensure that the decisions being made use the most current and accurate management information available. Even with this sort of information, managers will make stupid decisions from time to time, but at least the odds of making poor decisions drops precipitously as the quality of project information improves. Indeed, as all levels of management become acclimated to an environment where accurate cost and schedule performance information is disseminated quickly, the performance of the overall organization improves dramatically. I've seen it happen dozens of times, but I've also seen top-performing companies enter into sharp decline after achieving a high level of proficiency in project management. That's why I have structured this book the way I have.

But how does essential project management information get into the hands of decision makers? And, once delivered, how can that information stream be kept alive and flourishing?

This book was written to address these questions. Part 1 will review common, but futile tactics used to try to advance project management and reveal why they don't work. After deconstructing these tactics, Part 2 will show the technical approach with the most promise, and Part 3 will discuss the hazards involved in furthering project management within the organization, even with the optimal technical approach, as well as those things that can unravel the progress that the advanced project management office has attained.

CHAPTER 1

Leveraging Organizational Power

Messenger: "We win again!"
General: "That is good! But what is best in life?"
Warrior: "The open steppe, fleet horse, a falcon on your wrist, the wind in your hair!"
General: "Wrong! Conan, what is best in life?"
Conan: "To crush your enemies, see them driven before you, and to hear the lamentations of the women!"
General: "That is good!"

—Conan the Barbarian

I once headed up a project management office that included a former soldier among the project control engineers. Whenever he was frustrated by some work package manager who had failed to provide the needed baseline information or was slow in sending along the end-of-month status, he would storm into my office, seething.

"Michael!" he would start, "You need to get in there, and tell these guys that they *have* to provide this data!"

"I understand you're frustrated, but I don't think my powers of coercion will help in this situation."

"Well, then, you've got to get John (program director) to tell them they have to comply! You managers need to . . . (at this point this fellow employed a slang term which means, in essence, to acquire a backbone)!"

I completely sympathized with this fellow's aggravation. But in the final analysis, he had become ensnared in a common trap—the idea that, every time some organization had failed to advance its project management capability, it was due to some lack of organizational commitment. The eagerness or reluctance to engage in the so-called coercive strategies to advance any capability, including project management, is not a barometer of the odds of success. The success or failure of any attempt to implement project management is entirely predicated on the selection of the most appropriate technical approach and then preventing non-technical factors (such as politics) from derailing it. As managers, we can't afford to indulge in the conceit that failure on our part is due to lack of backing from the higher-ups. It is simply not the case that upper management can make all of your implementation problems go away with a wave of the hand (or a signature on a document, as we will see later). Once you have allowed yourself to fall into such a trap, your job only becomes more difficult.

I once heard about a study that revealed that almost two thirds of managers who are fired are not dismissed because they showed up to work late or failed to execute their jobs correctly. They are fired simply because someone did not like them. If you attempt to employ the coercive strategies in furthering the organization's project management capability, it's usually because that capability isn't advancing on its own. So, if it's not advancing on its own, there must be some form of residual organizational resistance. This resistance is a normal and predictable part of any organization, not some wrongheaded aberration. As such, it can be managed. Managers who routinely employ the coercive strategies will always sacrifice some level of popularity, and sacrificing popularity is the action most likely to derail their jobs, if not careers. So, let's take these two facts together:

1. The person who is forcing project management tactics upon a reluctant organization should expect an erosion of popularity within that organization, and
2. Lack of popularity within the organization leads to job loss.

Now is it clear why executive-level management is often less than thrilled to lead the vanguard in forcing the use of project management techniques and tools?

One of the most fascinating aspects of the coercive approach is that many managers simply cannot conceive of any other way of promoting a capability—any capability. As battles of wills become more personal, personal agendas begin to trump the technical agenda of the organization. Those maneuvering about the smoke-filled cloak room, wielding daggers and giving sideways glances become successful at the expense of the company's true contributors. I will address the dangers of political machinations to the PMO in a later chapter. For now, suffice to say that adapting the coercive strategies in advancing project management has the bitter consequence of providing an environment where the basest, most duplicitous elements of the organization can thrive at the expense of everyone else.

Now, having said all that, there are actually times when the coercive strategies can work. But even these successes, as rare as they are, tend to be short-lived and, when the inevitable collapse comes, the organization is typically less well-off than it had been before the attempted implementation. A prime example of this is a project management information system implementation attempt by a large United States government organization during the early 1990s. This particular organization was spending hundreds of millions of dollars every year to perform project work across the country. Recognizing the need for a comprehensive cost and schedule management information system, they developed a software tool that performed basic funding, milestone, and cost management functions. Each of the organization's sites—about 20 in number—had a copy of the software and would enter budget, actual cost, earned value (EV), and funding information into it. On a set schedule, these files would be copied and sent to the organization's headquarters, where they were processed into reports that showed how each of the projects in the portfolio were performing. A monthly teleconference would review the information, site by site, project by project, with an additional quarterly meeting added to address problem areas with higher levels of department management. Given the level of technology for the time, the implementation of this system was a remarkable achievement, and I have, to this day, a great deal of respect for those who pulled it off. It had only one fatal flaw: its implementation was based on the coercive strategies.

The offices of the various sites were required to participate in the teleconferences and meetings where the cost and schedule performance information was disseminated and reviewed. Failure to comply would receive the immediate attention of a high-ranking member of the department's management team and might endanger funding. For a couple of years, the entire portfolio complied. But then something interesting happened: (at least) one site's manager began to argue that the performance reports should not be produced. He was, shall we say, recalibrated, but then another site manager began to agitate for quarterly, rather than monthly, reviews. What was happening is typical of implementations using the coercive strategies: individual players were seeking ways to opt out. They knew that a frontal assault—coming right out and arguing against the overall system on principal—was an untenable option. Instead, they pushed back against the edges, the periphery of the system. Other sites began to do likewise, and in short order, the entire system was being opposed in its practical application. The death knell sounded when new management in the organization—who were not as familiar with earned value management systems (EVMSs) in general and this system in particular—came on the scene, and stopped insisting on full compliance. Almost immediately, a few major sites citing various, vacuous reasons stopped participating in the teleconferences and ceased supplying information via the system. With major pieces of the portfolio missing, the system no longer supplied key decision makers with the broad-based information they needed, and the system quickly fell into disrepute. Once this particular system was no longer used, the residual hostility towards it effectively blocked any adequate successor from being installed for some time, and during that time the organization's decision makers lost their ability to assess the cost and schedule performance of its entire portfolio. Of course, those who initiated the actions that led to the system's downfall did not admit that they were eliminating a key management capability. Rather, their arguments were consistently along the lines of promoting the capability of alternative information systems to assess and report on cost and schedule performance of the projects making up the portfolio. These arguments, though, were demonstrably false, since the earned value and critical path methodologies are the only means to assess cost and schedule performance of project work, and these methodologies were notably absent from the rival systems. Nevertheless, these assertions, as shallow as they were, carried the day, and what had been a remarkable, broad-based implementation success was allowed to fade off into the sunset.

What's important to note about this story is that in assessing lessons learned, the temptation is to blame the behavior of the organization. The problem was not in the organization, it was in the technical approach used in the implementation. The coercive strategies do not work, at least not in the long term. And when they fail, it will *always* appear to be the fault of the organization. W. Edward Deming once estimated that performance within the organization arises from a combination of workers' effort (15%) and the system within which they work (85%). Management is responsible for the system. If we take this assessment at face value, then implementation failures are 15% the fault of the organization and 85% the fault of management—or, in this case, the technical approach (or system) used by management. In other words, the behavior of the organization was perfectly understandable and predictable—it was the managerial approach that created the source of the frustration and failure associated with the effort.

I've offered the coerced EVMS story as one example, but the frustrations stemming from failed attempts to employ one of the coercive strategies are legion. At a project management leadership seminar I attended, the instructor encouraged the participants to write down the one, biggest problem they perceived to be within their organizations. One senior manager wrote that his organization's biggest problem was its reluctance to embrace and employ project management techniques in their work, and the rest of the room roundly agreed. During the next break, I approached this fellow and asked him if the problem really was as he articulated, or, perhaps, might it be that the technical approach to implementing project management was the wrong one for that organization? Based on his reaction, it was clear that that thought had never even occurred to him.

Never.

In the arena of implementation, the financial accountants (one of my favorite targets in my "Variance Threshold" column in *PM Network*) actually have a leg up on all other managers. After all, if anyone attempts to not do as the accountants say, they are, in all probability, committing a crime, specifically, fraud. In those cases, it's not the organization that's leveraging organizational power; it's the government, who collects tax revenue based on the execution of generally accepted accounting principles (GAAP). Anyone caught committing fraud is, of course, fired, if not tried, convicted, and jailed. With this juggernaut backing them up, the accountants (and all other resource managers, for that matter) never have to concern themselves with *how* their techniques get adapted by the macro-organization. All naysayers are systemically marginalized, if not out-and-out removed, from the company. For anyone who opposes the resource managers' techniques that are not outside the law, their fallback argument is all encompassing—such opposition hurts profits or the "bottom line." The trendy push to analyze the return on investment (ROI) on implementing project management attempts to tap into the accountants' fallback position, but this, too, fails to work because of the fundamental difference between project management and asset management. As my professors drilled into my skull while I pursued my MBA, the purpose of all management actions is to "maximize shareholder wealth." Conversely, the purpose of project management is to meet the customers' goals of scope, time, and budget. To engage in a bit of hyperbole, the project manager couldn't care less if the copying machine should have been rented or purchased: this individual is only concerned with whether or not the machine will crank out the deliverables expected by the customer. If it does, it's good, and if it doesn't, it needs to be replaced by a better machine, rented or bought. Because project management is so fundamentally different from asset management, attempting to piggyback an implementation approach based on asset management principals fails to gain traction, and is often reduced to, well, begging.

The Gap

This gap between project management and asset management may explain why many managers simply can't comprehend any approach other than leveraging organizational power. They see their fellow managers on the other side of the management type divide pursue their information system objectives and receive sufficient participation (however grudging) to make the objectives happen. The project management office then puts forward the exact same approach—articulating their cooperation needs, documenting the particulars of their systems, and then expecting a similar response from the macro-organization . . . and the PMO's objectives just don't happen.

Professor Tom Peters has written several books and presentations ridiculing the results that come from "maximizing shareholder wealth" with single-minded zeal. However, even as he illustrates the problems endemic in exclusively employing resource management approaches, I am unaware of any analysis he has presented that shows why the resource management approach seems to reign supreme in the first place. The reason Professor Peters doesn't receive first-class treatment in expensive hotels, for example, (when that actually occurs) is because the hotels' employees are unaware that their boorish behavior towards prominent management authors is hurting their "bottom line." They haven't been trained in the art of satisfying the customers' expectations of scope, cost, and schedule—in short, they're simply not project managers. While complaining entertainingly about the frustrations that arise from organizations focused on "maximizing shareholder wealth" provides interesting reading, the project management professional will receive no help with implementing project management from reading *In Search of Excellence.*

I've had several opportunities to observe what happens when strata of pro-project management executives are inserted into an organization where project management techniques have not been widely adopted, and the results are always the same. The new executives will express disgust that the benighted organization is sooooo backwards in project management capability, and then will leverage any and all of their power and influence to *make* people adapt their new approaches. These executives are invariably frustrated and will blame their lack of progress on the recalcitrance of others in the company. This frustration grows, and in those areas where they *can* punish others, morale quickly decreases. As turnover increases and projects encounter difficulties that could have been avoided, frustration increases and morale plummets—it's a vicious circle. And all the while, the techniques of project management assume a negative association throughout the company, further reducing the odds of widespread adoption. Finally, some major project fails so badly that a dramatic change in the organization takes place—assimilation, takeover, bankruptcy—and the people who attempted to leverage organizational power to implement project management never seem to realize it was this very approach that led to the disaster in the first place.

But for those managers who worked their way up in the project management arena and have then attained some level of authority and prominence, the notion that their hard work, education, and accomplishments would land them in a situation where their new "underlings" *must* obey them is only natural. It's *their turn,* after all. And when they, like their predecessors, fail, well, it was the fault of the organization!

No, it was their technical approach. The coercive strategies do not work, at least not in the long term.

Chapter Summary

While exerting authoritative power is a reflexive behavior when attempting to advance project management capabilities in an organization, it almost never works. The identification of the most appropriate technical approach is what's needed, not more coercion. Even in those instances where the coercive strategies work, it's never long term. Project management specialists may perceive that our asset-managing cousins, the accountants, can implement their techniques via appeals to the law and the bottom line, but PMO personnel don't have this kind of leverage and should not attempt to emulate their approaches. In those situations where leveraging organizational power and influence does not advance project management maturity (virtually every time), look at it objectively rather than simply attributing it to the recalcitrance of the host organization or some vague assessment of the time it takes to change the organization's "culture." It's all in the technical approach.

CHAPTER 2

Training and Certification

The other animal in my life, of course, is the Pinto I ride on *Bonanza*. His name is Cochise, and he's nuts. He hates all horses. No one can ride either in front of him or behind him. If there's a horse in back of him he kicks, and if there's one in front of him, he bites. That's why you usually see us riding abreast. The trouble with the horse is that he's only bold when I'm mounted. When no one is riding him, he's timid. He's been trained to rear up, and this looks great, even if it does make me look like the Lone Ranger. I just wish he wouldn't rear on my lines.

—Michael Landon

This chapter has the potential to be the most controversial chapter in the book, since project management training is a big industry and tended to by some of the most brilliant minds in the field. I must admit that it is obvious that a broad-based project management implementation is impossible without knowledgeable people in key positions to make things happen. But it is at least equally obvious that simply being trained in something does not compel us to do that thing. Many people are trained in cardio-pulmonary resuscitation (CPR), but how many of us have ever used it? My teenage son is a lifeguard at a city pool, and he's been trained in many first aid and rescue techniques. With the exception of city employees sent to test the lifeguards, he has *never* used any of this training—and he's a lifeguard! For further proof that training does not irrevocably lead to performance, consider that virtually all of us have been trained to do the following things:

- Don't speed while driving,
- Use turn signals,
- Don't talk on cell phones while driving,
- Don't jaywalk,
- Use safety goggles when working with power tools, and
- Use the rail when negotiating a staircase.

Even if we follow these axioms religiously, we're aware that most people don't. Why then would we assume that being trained in project management techniques automatically leads to the use of these techniques?

Training serves as an enabler. Without it, you won't be able to execute any system you happen to install, so it's clearly a key component. But in the realm of project management implementation, while training enables the organization to adopt these techniques, it does not drive or compel their use. This being the case, the type of training that your organization should pursue turns on a simple question: Will this training help put cost and schedule performance information into the hands of decision makers?

If the answer is clearly "yes," then get that training quickly. It's golden. The most notable examples of such training includes the earned value management courses offered by Humphreys and Associates, as well as those classes that teach how to use the more robust tools of the project management trade, such as Primavera Project Planner®. (In the interest of full disclosure, I consider Gary Humphreys to be a friend. That having been admitted, I have personally witnessed organizations reaping huge benefits from engaging Mr. Humphrey's organization and materials.)

Conversely (and this is where I stand to draw the most heat), take an honest assessment of your implementation goals and ask yourself, does spending training dollars on individuals pursuing professional certifications advance the technical agenda?

Professional credentials do not guarantee risk-free employees. Not every project will be successful because you employ a credentialed project manager. A credential does not even mean that the project manager practices certain or proper procedures. They may have the experience and education necessary to obtain the credential and may even have the knowledge and abilities to answer exam questions correctly. But a credential does not mean that the individual will practice project management under the ethical code they agreed to uphold or that they will practice according to the policies, procedures or cultural nuances of your organization.

Another unfortunate manifestation of focusing on improving the capabilities of the individuals on the project team as a means of advancing project management is the creation of internal certification programs. I have never seen a single one of these programs work, although I have witnessed several attempts. Much of the time these attempts are propagated by some individual who perceives that his or her experience, education, or certification is superior to some of those who are ahead of this individual in the organization. To compensate, this person will try to revamp the get-ahead criteria to more closely adhere to their own resumes. Invariably internal certification programs will present themselves as some sort of evaluation matrix for assessing fitness for assignment as a project manager or head of a PMO. Similar to the professional societies' certification programs, points are assigned based on education and experience, and these points indicate whether or not a candidate is qualified for any specific assignment.

In the world of project management implementation, two aspects are important when dealing with the top decision makers in the organization:

1. Nothing about what you are attempting to implement may impact their latitude in taking managerial actions, and
2. They must never be under the impression that anything you are doing is going to require them to work harder or to undertake a potentially unpopular initiative.

Internal certification has the unhappy characteristic of doing both. An internal certification program would inhibit upper management's latitude in assigning project managers and PMO personnel, since they may be forced to observe the rules on who may or may not get the most desirable assignments. And since the limiting of managerial actions is rarely seen as a good thing among managers, pushing that type of program will almost certainly make the person doing the pushing somewhat unpopular.

Part of the reason for the popularity of using training as a driver for implementation stems from the halcyon days of project management implementation—the 1970s. The United States Department of Defense (DOD) issued guidance—most notably, DOD 7000.10 and DOD 7000.20—that stipulated the use of scope, cost, and schedule management techniques and output. Known collectively as the cost/schedule control systems criteria (C/SCSC), these thorough requirements brooked no dissent. If a contractor could not demonstrate compliance with 42 criteria of baselining, accounting, and earned value and critical path analysis, then that contractor could receive no new business from the DOD. Since doing project management correctly was a condition of staying in business, implementation of these techniques took on an impetus that had been previously enjoyed only by the accountants. When the United States Department of Energy (DOE) was first formed during the Carter administration, they also mandated the use of project management techniques as a condition for doing business through them in the releasing of DOE Order 2250.1. Since the driver question had already been answered, it was left to the contractors to simply train their managers how to comply.

But then a funny thing happened on the way to project management nirvana. In the early 1980s, some of the larger U.S. government contractors began to complain about the difficulty in passing a C/SCSC audit. With literally millions of dollars riding on the often subjective opinions of audit teams that were sometimes partially composed of the target organization's competitors, the necessity of using project management techniques to manage cost and schedule performance came under attack. The DOE issued revised requirements citing a "graded approach" (more on this later) that represented a retreat from performing earned value and critical path analysis as a condition of doing business, essentially removing the driver behind project management implementation. I guess those managers insisting that a comprehensive training program will deliver more mature project management across the organization didn't get that memo or weren't paying attention. No longer would project management advancement occur automatically once the staff was sufficiently trained. But, in a turn of events that must have B.F. Skinner smiling from the great beyond, the learned behavior would be repeated over and over, even when the expected rewards ceased.

Training fails to further project management maturity because it does not induce participation, the key characteristic needed to further project management maturity. Competence in project management can be taught or trained, participation cannot.

Chapter Summary

Training programs can act as enablers of advancing project management maturity, but they cannot serve as drivers. Being trained to do a thing does not necessarily mean that the trainee will do that thing, no matter how good the trainer, facilities, curriculum, etc. The key ingredient in furthering project management techniques lies in obtaining participation from the organization. While the level of available expertise is an important factor, it's not the key factor. At one time, when using project management techniques was a condition of business, the only missing piece was training but those days are no more. The consultants who learned the trade during that time will often carry with them the dangerous illusion that training will drive project management maturity. It won't.

CHAPTER 3

Forcing the Tool

Tybalt: Mercutio, thou consortest with Romeo—
Mercutio: Consort! What, dost thou make us minstrels? And thou make minstrels of us, look to
hear nothing but discords. Here's my fiddlestick, here's that shall make you dance.

—Romeo and Juliet, Act 3, Scene 1

"Forcing the Tool" is the nickname I've given to the implementation technique of selecting
a particular software tool that performs some aspect of project management information
either earned value or critical path or both and attempting to leverage organizational power to
compel its use. Unfortunately, this is a very common approach. The previous example of the
government agency's earned value software was a variant of forcing the tool. This approach has
two very powerful forces arrayed against it: those problems inherent in leveraging organizational
power (as described in Chapter 1), plus those issues surrounding the introduction of any management
information stream, namely, the selection of the most appropriate platform(s), identification of the
source(s) of raw data, roles and responsibilities, and training both operators and consumers in its use.

The Old Economies-of-Scale Argument

The use of this tactic is almost always furthered using the argument that it's more efficient to have
one software platform processing the project management information than it is to have several.
From computer support to training, this argument is essentially appealing to the benefits that can
be derived from economies of scale. The problem here, though, is that calculating the benefits from
economies of scale has to do with efficiency not effectiveness. Only when a process is already in
place and functioning is it appropriate to evaluate it with respect to its most and least efficient
aspects in order to assess areas for improvement. Where the desired capability does not exist at all,
the economies of scale argument is logically invalid, and any manager who knows enough about
such an analysis ought to know that. And yet this argument is invariably used to justify the forcing
the tool approach, and further used to bludgeon those opposed into silence.

Another major problem with the economies-of-scale argument has to do with the nature of
implementation efforts in their early stages. Latitude, or the ability to adapt to diverse tastes and
dynamic circumstances in delivering information to decision makers, is absolutely essential to
implementation efforts in the early going. That's the beauty of retaining the option of processing

your PMO information through a spreadsheet—a spreadsheet can show information in so many different ways that you're almost certainly going to be able to adjust to any format request you receive. Such a capability is markedly absent from almost all of the off-the-shelf project management software packages.

Which Tool?

There are many software tools available to process project management information, and selecting the right one is fraught with hazards all by itself. The key to evaluating the most appropriate platform lies with an undeniable truth about management information systems: all valid MISs have the following basic structure:

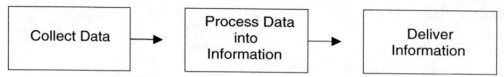

Figure 3-1.   Basic management information structure.

Collect Data. This step is performed in accordance with some sort of discipline. For example, accountants collect data on purchases and incomes and rates and hours worked in order to process financial information. Project managers and project controllers collect the data needed to create work breakdown structures, cost and schedule baselines, and the status of the activities and tasks that make up the project.

Process the Data into Information. This step is performed using some sort of methodology. In the accountants' case, they use double-entry bookkeeping methods to process their data into balance sheets and profit-and-loss statements. Project managers and controllers use the earned value and critical path methods to process cost and schedule performance information.

Deliver the Information. This step requires more than stuffing an in-box. The information must be presented in such a way as to be immediately usable by the organization's decision makers. Unless they are already advanced in project management techniques, this will require that the project management information stream be sent along in a format that is highly intuitive. Mostly for this reason the forcing the tool tactic is doomed to failure. In the earliest phases of introducing project management, the eventual end users are often new to the concepts. Imagine trying to explain a balance sheet to someone who knows little or nothing about accounting! And yet, most of the software packages that perform project management information analysis yield outputs such as Gantt charts, PERT charts, or even cost performance reports (format 1), which are guaranteed to induce what P.J. O'Rourke calls MEGO (My Eyes Glaze Over). The off-the-shelf packages simply lack the adaptability to, for lack of a better term, dumb-down the output so that high-ranking project management neophytes can readily understand the information being presented to them. One corporation that promotes an off-the-shelf EVMS runs a series of advertisements in trade magazines in a conversational format, where the characters sneer at the practice of using spreadsheets to process project controls information. In true forcing-the-tool form, they go on to use the economies-of-scale argument for their particular software package, but the truth here is that spread-sheets (most notably Microsoft Excel®) can do a very adequate job of representing earned value data in a vast array of highly intuitive formats, a trick that few, if any, of the off-the-shelf earned value packages can do themselves.

The Black Box Syndrome

When I took the Certified Cost Consultant (CCC) examination from the then American Association of Cost Engineers (AACE), one of the two-hour tests covered the critical path methodology (CPM). They presented some two dozen activities with their durations and schedule logic, and the test taker had to lay out the entire network, perform a forward pass and a backward pass, find the critical path, and calculate float. As you can imagine, this took considerable time. Then the follow-on questions were similar to "Activity D-5 changes in duration from 45 days to 75 days. What does this do to the schedule?" The obvious answer was "It changes it in such a way that I've got to redo all my &%$# calculations, you jerks!" Of course, I did not answer in such a way, and instead recalculated the whole network. There were several follow-on questions along these lines.

I understood where they were coming from. No self-respecting project controls engineer is without the ability to manually analyze a critical path scheduling network. But many in this profession, and in all likelihood within the PMO, are unaware how to manually create and maintain either a critical path network or an earned value management system. This is largely due to the existence of software packages that perform the essential processing of the raw data into usable information automatically, and all the project controls engineer *has* to do is enter the data and enact certain processing parameters, and they're there. This convenience helps fuel the economies-of-scale argument as well, since it's far easier to buy 20 copies of Primavera Project Planner® than it is to train 20 project controls engineers how to perform in the exact same way 100% of the time, all of the data processing that Primavera® can do. But this convenience also leads to a very real trap that I call the black box syndrome.

If the software package being pushed as the centerpiece of a forcing the tool approach is off-the-shelf, then the broad range of information that the PMO needs to deliver to the organization's decision makers will tend to narrow down to the capability of the software. Primavera®, for example, is a robust critical path methodology tool (it is, in fact, my favorite). But delivering earned value information in highly intuitive ad hoc formats is not its long suit and being able to do just that is absolutely critical to the young PMO's success (more on this later). I once had the unhappy experience of working with a person who was an expert in entering data and manipulating the parameters of schedules in Primavera Project Planner®, but had come to the conclusion that if Primavera® couldn't do it, then it wasn't a worthwhile piece of project management information. Rather than debate the stance logically, this individual simply set up a sort of Primavera® cult where the worth of any project controls engineer simply *had* to be evaluated solely on the individual's level of expertise with that particular software package. This was one of the nastiest forcing-the-tool implementations I have ever witnessed, combining as it did the worst aspects of black box syndrome with leveraging organizational clout, in this instance represented by the "subject matter expert" status assumed by this mistress of the black box. Not only did this particular PMO fail to provide its customers with the schedule and cost performance information they needed, but morale within the PMO cratered. Things only improved after this person had left town altogether.

Things only get worse if the black box syndrome features a homegrown software tool. The problem with homegrown software tools designed to process project management information is the exact opposite of the off-the-shelf tools. If the off-the-shelf tools lack flexibility, then their homegrown counterparts have too much. The part of the organization that is developing the project management information system will feel immense pressure to be all things to all information customers, which soon leads to the incorporation of invalid business practices in the software. I just happen to know of a current internationally marketed earned value management system that had its roots in a homegrown system. At one time (and perhaps even currently), this system allowed the user to calculate earned value information in one of 15 different ways. The ANSI standard for earned value recognizes only six. This system's remaining methods were, obviously enough to all but its developers, invalid but that didn't stop the company that developed this tool from using it as a centerpiece in a forcing-the-tool blitzkrieg. Interestingly enough, even though the developers were subcontractors, they also initiated a quasi-subject matter expert caste system predicated on level of expertise with the software tool. In the off-the-shelf example, the information became next to useless because it couldn't be delivered in formats sufficiently intuitive for the decision makers. In this homegrown instance, the information became useless because of the corruption of the methods used to process the data into information. In both cases, there was a massive negative impact to PMO morale.

Essentially, the lack of latitude that restricts the PMO that has elected to standardize on one or two software packages in the early stages of an implementation proves crippling.

Chapter Summary

Even though the tactic of forcing the tool is extremely common, it just doesn't work. It has the unhappy characteristic of combining the worst elements of the leveraging-organizational-power approach with those problems inherent in establishing any new management information stream. A particularly insidious variant of forcing the tool includes the black box syndrome, which not only fails to deliver the desired advancements in project management, it also tends to completely wreck morale within the project management office.

CHAPTER **4**

Procedures and Guides

Obie came in with the 27, 8 × 10 color glossy pictures with circles and arrows and a paragraph on the back of each one, sat down. Man came in said, "All rise." We all stood up, and Obie stood up with the 27, 8 × 10 color glossy pictures, and the judge walked in sat down with a seeing eye dog, and he sat down, we sat down. Obie looked at the seeing eye dog, and then at the 27, 8 × 10 color glossy pictures with circles and arrows and a paragraph on the back of each one, and looked at the seeing eye dog. And then at 27, 8 × 10 color glossy pictures with circles and arrows and a paragraph on the back of each one and began to cry . . .

—Arlo Guthrie, *Alice's Restaurant*

Is there anything in the world easier to ignore than a document? Put another way, if a document could induce the use of project management techniques in an organization, why hasn't such a document been written already (including this one)?

Those documents that are influential—why are they? The most influential books contain ideas and assertions that are so insightful and true that they enable us to live our lives better than if we were to eschew such ideas. All others are simply reference books. So into which category do you suppose your company's project management guidance falls? Yes, the adaptation of project management techniques will enable your organization to execute its technical agenda far more effectively than if it doesn't, but this is hardly a universally accepted idea. Since project management aficionados can't presume that our guides and procedures will be recognized as an advantage giver on a par with *The Art of War*, those procedures are, effectively, little more authoritative than a thesaurus on the typical manager's desk.

Those who support the generation of procedures and guides to further project management implementation are legion. Indeed, I have never encountered an organization that prided itself on its ability to perform project management techniques that did not insist on thorough documentation. But I can't help but wonder exactly how these documents further implementation. What's the exact scenario where a trade manual turns a project-management-rejecting organization into a project management performer? Essentially, the success scenario comes down to a project management champion confronting the rejecter on his rejection, citing chapter and verse of the procedure and threatening to expose the interloper to the procedure violation police. This raises the question: Who constitutes the procedure violation police?

Are the procedure violation police composed of the customers? Having one part of the organization go to the customer to tell on another part of the organization is politically suicidal. Are the procedure violation police members of the organization? Internal auditors, perhaps? What really happens when the organization's internal auditors write up a manager? Does he receive a demotion? A scolding? Anything at all?

It has been my experience that even in those cases where a project was so horrifically mismanaged that it incurred tens of millions of dollars in overruns, and the proximate cause of such a project disaster was the absence of an earned value management system, those who were responsible for eliminating the EVMS are never held accountable for such actions. As a rule, those managers who most effectively shoot down legitimate attempts to implement project management techniques never receive their comeuppance. Never. There are simply too many pseudo-intellectual arguments available to cover their collective backsides. And, at the end of the day, no eat-your-peas documentation can possibly eradicate that.

I actually attended a project management seminar where one of the featured speakers was a man whose major government research project overran by millions and millions of dollars. Was he there to discuss where he had gone wrong; to evaluate his jaw-dropping idiotic performance in the project management arena in order to warn the rest of us not to repeat the same mistake? No—he was there to *boast* about his team's earned value management system, the same system which had been installed *after* the main part of the cost disaster had already taken place! I swear I am not making this up. At the earliest stages of this project's execution, its management team made it a point to announce that they would not be engaging "classical" earned value or critical path systems, because they were so much more "advanced" in their management approach, don't you know. Months later, they were submitting baseline change proposals (BCP) that requested *double* the budget and time allotted in the first baseline. Within a year after *that* BCP, they submitted another again doubling the budget and duration. And the killer is that both the customer organization and the performing organization had multiple procedures, guides, and, yes, requirements documented that were aimed at preventing this exact scenario from unfolding. The management team:

- Ignored the documents,
- Incurred massive cost overruns and schedule delays,
- In the ultimate act of closing the barn door after the horses had escaped, installed an EVMS *after* the overruns had been realized, and
- Not only failed to be punished or discredited in any way, but went on to make presentations at project management conferences about how well they were "doing" earned value.

In what must have been a shocking turn of events for the documents-driving-project management-implementation camp, the reams of printed pages did not, in fact, grow arms and legs, march en masse towards the guilty PMO, and enforce the rules listed in their pages, human-chain like. I am somewhat comfortable in asserting that this has never happened and will never happen. The only way that documents, procedures, guides, even the vaunted *A Guide to the Project Management Body of Knowledge* (PMBOK® Guide—Third Edition) can be of any use whatsoever is if it is rolled up into a usable club and wielded by someone who is trying to leverage organizational power to force compliance with project management's "best practices," which is another approach that doesn't work, by the way (see Chapter 1).

But hope springs eternal. There's a sense that, if only the project management guidance or procedure is signed by enough of a high-ranking personage, then everyone *must* acknowledge and obey it. But even two years after the United States Department of Energy issued its Order 413.3, which stipulated that major projects must have earned value management systems that are "consistent" with ANSI/EIA-748-A-1998 Earned Value Management Systems, a significant chunk of major programmatic work remains free from any real EVMS reporting requirements. Yet, when DOE 413N was first issued, several prominent project management gurus hailed it as the "project controllers full employment act of 2004." Still, a significant chunk of major programmatic work within the DOE remains free from any real EVMS reporting requirements. Meanwhile, executives with the Association for the Advancement of Cost Engineering International (AACE International) made progress in getting certain state legislators to support the idea that major projects should have their estimates verified in some way by a Certified Cost Engineer (CCE) or Certified Cost Consultant (CCC), with AACEI being the main certification agency. The last time I checked, there were no real requirements for major state projects to fully embrace cost engineering reporting requirements. Then, when the Sarbanes-Oxley Act of 2002 passed, there was much excitement from the earned value practitioners that its best-business-practice-or-else components could be used to drive earned value compliance, and I attended several seminar paper presentations that boldly predicted that the EV lovers had won, game, set, and match. Still, a significant chunk of major programmatic work within . . . oh, you know the rest. The short answer is that it didn't happen.

No, if project management or cost engineering techniques are going to make inroads into your organization, it won't be because someone wrote a document that says so (or, in the common vernacular, says it "shall"). The implementation burden will not be magically lifted off of the shoulders of PMO personnel by document-preparers, and it's a complete waste of time to wish otherwise.

Chapter Summary

Another common failed approach to advancing project management techniques is the thorough documentation of the desired processes and outcomes. The practice of generating such documents may actually prove detrimental in those instances where it dissipates the PMO's energy in a futile effort. Not even guidance from customers or governmental agencies will effectively further project management maturity, and the anticipation that it will accomplish that will end in frustration and failure.

CHAPTER 5

Consultants

Mr. Anemone: Mr. Chigger. So, you want to learn to fly.

Mr. Chigger: Yes.

Mr. Anemone: Right, well, up on the table, arms out, fingers together, knees bent . . .

Mr. Chigger: No, no, no.

Mr. Anemone: Up on the table! Arms out, fingers together, knees bent, now, head well forward. Now, flap your arms. Go on, flap, faster. . . faster. . . faster. . . faster, faster, faster, faster—now jump! Rotten. Rotten. You're no bloody use at all. You're an utter bloody wash-out. You make me sick, you weed!

Mr. Chigger: Now look here. . .

Mr. Anemone: All right, all right. I'll give you one more chance, get on the table. . .

Mr. Chigger: Look, I came here to learn how to fly an aeroplane.

Mr. Anemone: A what?

Mr. Chigger: I came here to learn how to fly an aeroplane.

Mr. Anemone: Oh, 'an aeroplane'. Oh, I say, we are grand, aren't we? 'Oh, oh, no more buttered scones for me, mater. I'm off to play the grand piano'. 'Pardon me while I fly my aeroplane.' Now get on the table!

—Monty Python's Flying Circus, episode 16

Some of my best friends are consultants, so I'd better tread lightly in this chapter. The problem with consultants, however, is reminiscent of a quote from Dr. Deming, who said that 85% of the organizations' problems arise from the system implemented by management and 15% arise from the efforts of the workers. With that assertion in mind, ask yourself who pays for the consultants?

Consultants, too, fall into the trap of assuming that leveraging organizational power is the key to implementing project management. To many of them, the only question left to answer is where, exactly, to lean? To assess the answer to that question, they have a plethora of their infernal checklists that are often strongly reminiscent of the 42 critera from the C/SCSC. ("Hey, isn't that checklist you're using from DOD 7000.20?" At this point John Wayne should show up and deliver the line, "Well, it isn't very diff'rent from it either, is it, pilgrim?") These consultants will then proceed to beat the host organization's managers over the head with their project management templates, or ways of managing that worked for the consultants back when they were in their intellectual formative years (invariably during the days of C/SCSC). They then issue condemnatory findings against those in the organization who they perceive to oppose their recommendations. Organizational power is easier to wield when you don't have to pay for the negative consequences of your recommendations. It's sort of like gambling with other people's money. But consultants, by their nature, do not have an ongoing relationship with their clients. This leaves them at liberty to criticize, challenge, and condemn with impunity, a luxury not enjoyed by those who are in a long-term relationship with the company, that is, employees. Essentially, the consultants have all of the problems associated with leveraging organizational power (Chapter 1) with the additional problem of not being as familiar with the organization as those they end up condemning. They basically have two strikes against them before they even enter the batter's box.

Some consultants have an awareness of this aspect of the nature of their business and work hard to eliminate the more subjective aspects of their analysis and recommendations. I applaud these people. It has been my experience, however, that this sort of consultant is rare indeed, and that the vast majority of them approach their client organizations with a template. If the particulars of this template are not observed or respected, then the findings and condemnations start flowing, nuance and unique circumstances be damned.

One of the finest project management specialists I have ever met is a man named David Hampton. He is a triathlon aficionado and has a runner's body, a keen wit, and a genuine desire for doing things right—in this case, project management. Mr. Hampton had worked tirelessly within his organization to influence management to adopt and adhere to project management techniques and had actually made significant progress, when some consultants descended on one of his larger projects to initiate a "review." As fate would have it, those performing the review were known to me from co-participation in various seminars and symposiums. They struck me as petty and narrow-minded, but I suppose they had sufficient certifications on their résumés, and so they conducted their review. I talked to him soon afterwards, and he was devastated.

"What happened?" I asked.

"Well, we didn't have a completely up-to-date resource dictionary on the widget project and got dinged for that."

"'Dinged' how? Did they issue a corrective action request?"

"No, it came back as a recommended practice, but at one point one of them looked at me and asked 'How can you sleep at night?'"

These tyrannical PMO director wannabes had walked into the review with their own little template about how project management ought to be done and spent virtually no time at all getting to know their target. How they must have commended themselves afterwards, pretending to be the agents of virtuous and insightful management practices, when all they could do is make the actual performers look bad in front of higher management. And, if you so-called consultants are reading this book and recognize yourselves (they never do), do us all a favor: go home and leave everyone else alone, would you?

Whenever you hear of consultants coming in to review your project management systems, ask yourself: Whose agenda is being furthered here? Because I can almost guarantee that *someone* is making a political statement or thrust, and the consultants are there for one purpose and one purpose only: to provide a fig leaf of technical competence over this ploy. Far from helping advance the maturity of project management information systems, the hiring of consultants is at best neutral in such an endeavor and, at worst, actually works against it.

Chapter Summary

Back in the day when project management techniques were a prerequisite for working major government projects, forced implementation was easy, and the typical consultant only needed one or two major procurements under his or her belt in order to be considered an expert in the field. That has all changed, but many consultants are unaware and have assumed the personae of imperialistic scolds who can actually do more damage than good in your attempts to further project management.

CHAPTER 6

Inertia and the Need for Drivers

"Lead me, follow me, or get out of my way."

—George S. Patton

Leadership is a knowable quality, but you wouldn't know that from much of what has been written about it. With some notable exceptions, like Michael D. Abrashoff's outstanding book *It's Your Ship,* much of what has been covered in texts on leadership address things like the whole silly debate about whether or not leaders are born or made or what personal characteristics make up a good leader. These discussions are simply a waste of time and intellectual energy. Consider that successful leaders have been known to be stubborn, while others have been known to be flexible; some leaders are extremely intelligent, while advanced intelligence in others seems to crowd out their leadership capacity. In the previous chapters we've reviewed approaches to implementation that do not work, and the crown jewel of the failed approaches has to be lack of leadership. Inertia—bodies at rest tending to stay at rest—can and will ruin any and all attempts to further project management capabilities within the organization. The antidote to inertia is leadership.

Successful managerial leadership requires the following three characteristics or behaviors:

1. A leader must be able to conceptualize the most appropriate technical agenda. This means that she has to have the competence—gained from education, experience, or both—to understand the task before her. Patton had to know how best to use infantry with mechanized forces to conquer territory before he could execute his agenda. I call this "the vision thing."

2. A leader must be able to articulate his approach to accomplishing the technical agenda. This doesn't necessarily require advanced eloquence, especially if the technical agenda being pursued is commonly held to be the best approach. However, if what's being sold is not popular, such as persuading the last free nation in Europe to take on a totalitarian juggernaut in 1939, then the artful speech of a Winston Churchill becomes irreplaceable.

3. Finally, a leader must be willing to pursue the articulated technical agenda, alone, if necessary. Once again I'll refer to George Patton, who made it very clear that he was eager to take on the Axis armies himself. Conversely, those managers who are manifestly unwilling to execute the technical agenda themselves, but rather advise others on the behavior they ought to be adapting will never be considered true leaders. Keep in mind that this doesn't mean that only a general can attack an enemy, or only a prime minister can persuade others to

follow. History is full of Sergeant Yorks, who saw an opportunity, implemented his agenda (by himself, at first, but then with followers), and used the power of his two legs to carry it out.

Few things are more frustrating to workers than to waste time pursuing the wrong technical agenda. One of the ways workers will gauge whether or not the stated technical agenda is worth pursuing is how they perceive upper management's commitment to it. This reason alone is sufficient to introduce a large amount of resistance to change within the organization. Overcoming this resistance is what is required from the project management office, and it takes leadership. Specifically, the leader within the PMO must:

1. Know the best technical approach to implementing project management techniques and information systems. And, in case you haven't guessed it by now, if your technical approach is predicated on any (or all) of the previous chapters' tactics, you need to read the rest of this book.
2. Be able to articulate that approach in such a way that it is readily understandable by all. If your vision is so complicated or nuanced that the PMO staff can not readily understand it, it's probably fundamentally flawed.
3. Leverage their organizational and influential power to pursue the agenda. Note that we are not leveraging organizational power to force behavioral compliance—we're simply removing barriers to success that already exist within the organization. The leader must commit intellectual, energy, and, yes, emotional investment in the pursuit of the agenda.

The following chapters of this book will address the things that a project management office should do to make this kind of leadership happen. For now, suffice to say that inertia does exist within the organization, and only active leadership can overcome it.

Chapter Summary

Even though it's not entirely clear what characteristics make up a good leader, there's no question that some leadership ability will be needed in the PMO. Managerial leadership requires (1) Conceptualization: advanced knowledge in the field in order to conceptualize the best technical approach, (2) Articulation: the ability to clearly articulate to the team what that technical agenda is, and (3) Execution: a demonstrated willingness to pursue that agenda, alone if necessary.

CHAPTER 7

The Graded Approach

"Justice delayed is justice denied."

—William Ewart Gladstone

Sounds so reasonable, doesn't it? A *Graded Approach.* Oooooo. Because project management is so important, so crucial to get it right, and the rest of us in the organization, we're so backwards in this regard, we just can't take it on all at once, understand?

Management professor and fellow *PM Network* columnist Bud Baker once e-mailed me about one of my columns, "To Kill a PMO." Bud noted how, in his experience in the United States Air Force, that a common PMO-killing tactic was to stall project management progress with insincere cooperation. The tactic gained the name "the slow roll," and Bud ended his e-mail describing this trick with the sentence "The possibilities for creative destruction were endless."

Endless, indeed. This is where the graded approach derives its destructive power. It's like a paraphrase of "Justice delayed is justice denied," morphed to "Implementation delayed is implementation denied."

If you've never read guidance on how to implement using a graded approach, let me save you hours of mind-numbingly boring and intellectually vacuous tripe. They all say the same thing. The graded approach is a set of critera laid out for those parts of the project portfolio that must implement project management techniques and at what level. Problem is, when they state which projects *must* do project management, they also stipulate which ones don't. And wouldn't you know it? As soon as such guidance makes an appearance, virtually all of the projects can make some claim to belonging to the subset that doesn't have to do any project management at all! It's a miracle!

Does the guidance require *projects* to "do" project management? Well, we're a *program*, not a project! Work over $5 million must comply? Our program is a set of projects, and each of them is under the limit! Only high-risk programmatic work needs this level of scrutiny? Our risk analysis shows that we're low-risk! No matter what criterion are laid out for project work that must be managed as a project, the managers of that work will make a strong case for their work not meeting those criterions. It never fails.

In 1995 the United States DOE issued DOE Order 4700.1, *Project Management System,* which superceded DOE Order 2250.1D, *Cost and Schedule Control System Criterion. Project Management*

System introduced the graded approach, and its effects were devastating. Millions of dollars worth of programmatic work were suddenly free to avoid reporting performance against baselines, and the project overruns and delays that followed reflected the wrong-headedness of the graded approach. As the management difficulties mounted, a revision, 4700.5, which attempted to prevent "high-risk" projects from opting out of essential cost engineering practices, was issued. It didn't help, as the contractors' disingenuous project managers continued to claim the right to not integrate project management information systems, based on the criteria laid out in the graded approach documents.

To be fair, I readily concede the allure of the graded approach. It builds on many of the myths that this book has tried to overturn and simply extends them to their logical, anti-project management end. These myths include:

- Implementing an earned value management system is difficult, expensive, and time consuming. It isn't, unless you have some pseudo-intellectual buffoons adding layers and layers of complexity onto it.
- Any EVMS that is simple or easy to implement generates useless or even misleading information. This part of the graded approach myth is one of the most disingenuous. As discussed in other parts of this book, even a simple EVMS provides far more accurate, timely, and useful data than any of the alternatives offered up by the accountants or action item list aficionados.
- The widespread use of project management techniques in the macroorganization requires a "culture change," which takes a long time to accomplish. This is pure hokum, a transparent attempt to submerge overt objections to advancing project management into the swamp of muddle-headed, vaguely worded organizational behavior and performance jargon.
- Project management techniques are appropriate only for high-dollar or high-risk projects. These techniques are appropriate for any work where you care about its outcome. Besides, in most organizations the cumulative amount of the budgets of its "small" projects often dwarfs the sums of the budgets of the fewer "large" projects. Eliminating the largest part of the project portfolio from cost and schedule performance is a, well, stupid idea.

Deconstructing the myths that serve to prop up the absurdity of the graded approach is a good way to resist it, but the graded approach also fails in its utter essence which seeks to push forward the idea that project management information systems should not be broad-based. I have a theory, that all project managers perform earned value analysis at some point in their project, and the proof is in this: What project manager, upon hearing that his or her project has spent half of its budget, can avoid thinking "am I half done?" At that moment, a rudimentary earned value analysis has occurred. If the project manager tells anyone else about the results of his analysis, he has engaged in earned value reporting. Note that this is true even for very small projects. Since all project managers do earned value, I can't help but laugh at those managers who whine and caterwaul excessively about how their projects are so small they can't possibly be asked to "do" earned value. These so-called managers are simply exhibiting the vastness of their intellectual laziness when they reel off such objections.

Another way in which the graded approach proponents gain traction is when they blur the distinction between work that should be managed as a project and work that shouldn't. In reviewing all of the work performed by a given organization, a simple acid test for that work that should be managed as a project consists of asking the following questions:

- Does the work have discernible beginning and ending dates?
- Is there a product or a service being provided?
- Are resources dedicated to accomplishing articulated goals?
- Can the work's percent complete status be ascertained?

If the answers to these questions are "yes," then the work should be managed as a project. If the answers are "no," then it probably shouldn't. It really is that simple, but those opposed to project management implementation have a vested interest in muddying these waters. Without such a clear-eyed distinction about which parts of the portfolio are being captured in project management information systems, it's easy to waste time, money, and energy in the attempts to implement earned value and critical path systems where the information return isn't worth it. These attempts give fuel to the graded approach ninnies, who can then point to such failures as evidence that parts of the portfolio should be excluded from the project management systems being implemented. Technically that's right, but it's NOT right that *projects* should be excluded from the project management systems. Successful project management information systems must be broad-based, encompassing all legitimate project work. I address this in more detail in Part 2 of this book; for now, suffice to say that if any part of the project portfolio is allowed to opt out of participating in performance measurement systems, then most of the projects in the portfolio will attempt to follow suit. Before you know it, the entire implementation initiative will have come to a grinding halt, and it will remain in that condition until you can free yourself from the constraints of the graded approach.

Chapter Summary

The "graded approach" to implementing project management techniques across an organization or program office is one of the biggest frauds being perpetrated in the name of ideal practices in existence. So intellectually bankrupt is the graded approach that anyone within the PMO who even gives it lip service should be considered immediately suspect. The reasons for this are varied, but boil down to the graded approach representing an invalid technical approach structure, virtually inviting any and all of the other invalid approaches into the arena of ideas.

References

Project Management Institute, Inc. 2006. *The standard for portfolio management.* Newtown Square, PA: Project Management Institute.

Project Management Institute, Inc. 2006. *The standard for program management.* Newtown Square, PA: Project Management Institute.

Szilagyi, A. D., and Wallace, M. J. 1987. *Organizational Behavior and Performance,* 4th ed. London: Scott, Foresman and Company.

PM Network columns where I make fun of accountants include:

"Ancient PMBOK Manuscripts," *PM Network,* April 1998

"The Incontrovertible Rules of Project Management," *PM Network,* May 2000.

"Extreme Management Writing," *PM Network,* March 2002.

"Enemies List," *PM Network,* December 2002

"Planet of the CPAs," *PM Network,* September 2004

Abrashoff, M., 2002, *It's Your Ship,* Warner Books.

Peters, T. and Waterman, R., 1982, *In Search of Excellence,* Harper and Row.

Cleary, T. 1995, *Mastering the Art of War,* Shambhala.

Hatfield, M. "To Kill a PMO," *PM Network,* July 2007

PART 2

Tactics that Work

An inconvenience is only an adventure wrongly considered; an adventure is an inconvenience rightly considered.

—Gilbert Keith Chesterson

You will find that eschewing the tactics that don't work is only part of solving the problem of advancing project management within your organization. The main part of achieving success in this endeavor is to employ the technical approach that maximizes your chances of success and pursuing that with all of the strength, leverage, influence, and clout inherent in your position within your organization. Time is of the essence, no matter the amount of assurances you have received from higher-ups along the lines of their proffered patience and understanding of the size of the task before you. It's absolutely imperative that you demonstrate tangible successes in your progress towards project management implementation quickly, and that will only come from embracing the best possible technical approach to implementation and pursuing it with myopic zeal.

Put another way, the overarching component of your approach to implementing project management must be effectiveness over efficiency. Find out how to deliver systems and reports, and then figure out how to improve the process later—much later, if the process threatens to interfere with results. As Larry the Cable Guy says, "git 'er done."

What Kind of PMO Do You Have? What Kind Do You Want? And What's the Difference?

There are many types of organizations that call themselves a project management office, and they have varied placements within the macroorganization as well. Some PMOs are directly responsible for project work, while others serve as the line management axis and simply deploy their employees to those parts of the organization actually doing the work. Some PMOs report to the Chief Executive Officer (or equivalent), while others are placed within the same organization as the finance and accounting department (always a mistake). The mission of the PMO and its placement within the macroorganization has a direct bearing on your chances for success, as depicted in the following table:

Place/Mission	Directly Responsible for Project Work	Consults to Those Directly Responsible for Project Work	Provides PM Resources to Those Directly Responsible for Project Work
Higher Placement than the Accountants	Good shot at delivering on goals and expectations	Fraught with danger, but there's definitely a decent chance of success	If the accountant's organization is also in the deployed mode, you have a shot. Otherwise, get ready to bail.
Equal Placement to the Accountants	Decent shot at delivering and realizing goals.	Again, a decent shot at success, but you will have to be careful to keep the accountants in their place.	If the accountant's organization is also in the deployed mode, you have a shot. Otherwise, get ready to bail.
Beneath or Belonging to the Accountants	Absolutely hopeless, bail immediately	If the responsible organizations have a real appreciation for PM, you might pull this off.	Lotsa luck.

Some PMOs will have a combination of the missions listed in the table, while still others' placement in the macroorganization with respect to the accountants will be vague. But PMO personnel need to be aware that the nature of their mission, the approximate amount of organizational clout that they have to influence decisions, and the outcomes of managerial conflicts have a direct bearing on their odds of success. The successful PMO is one that has a realistic sense of where it is in the macroorganization, its limitations, and authorities. Hint: the PMO's actual placement within the organization is almost never accurately reflected in an organizational chart, and virtually all writings that purport to document formal roles and responsibilities (R&R) are essentially wish lists.

In summary, before you begin to undertake the tactics that actually work as listed in the subsequent chapters, have an unblinking, clear-eyed view of your operating parameters. Don't mistake the initial enthusiasm that accompanied the PMO's creation for unfailing organizational power, or you and your team will have an unnecessarily difficult and frustrating road ahead.

CHAPTER 8

Cooperation and Defection

The great difficulty of all schemes for leagues of nations and the like has been to find an effective sanction against nations determined to break the peace.

—Robert Cecil, 1st Viscount Cecil of Chelwood

There are many theoretical models in the business world for evaluating implementation efforts. There's DUME, which has the following steps:

- Define,
- Use,
- Measure, and
- Evaluate.

There's also IDEAL, which asserts that the steps associated with implementation are:

- Initiating,
- Diagnosing,
- Establishing,
- Acting, and
- Leveraging.

The famous Plan-Do-Check-Act (PDCA) model is self-explanatory, and, of course, the total quality management seven-step process includes:

- Assess,
- Educate,
- Identify customers,
- Create infrastructure,
- Write the vision,
- Write the policy, and
- Construct the strategic plan.

The Project Management Institute has developed the *Organizational Project Management Model (OPM3®),* and then there's Carnegie Mellon University's (CMU) famous Capability Maturity

Model (CMM®). Each of these models has its strengths and its shortcomings, but they all serve as yardsticks, structures that would prove useful in comparing the relative advancements in capabilities—in this case, project management capabilities. Of them all, my favorite is CMU's Software Engineering Institute's (SEI) Capability Maturity Model©. It just strikes me as the most prescient structure to use in developing a technical approach for improving project management capability within the macroorganization.

The capability maturity model sets its comparative stages as "levels," where the organization manifests certain behaviors. These levels include:

- Level 1: Initial. At Level 1, the organization's capability is chaotic. No standard exists, so each part of the organization is free to do its own thing, or nothing at all. Paradoxically, areas of advanced expertise can (and often do) exist within a CMM Level 1 organization, but, for the most part, no consistent, cohesive capability exists.
- Level 2: Repeatable. At this level, the capability being advanced is somewhat basic, but at least it's repeatable. Each part of the organization is performing the capability in the same way, using the same forms, techniques, and output.
- Level 3: Defined. Essentially, if the proverbial beer truck hits the "heroes" who got you to this point, the system doesn't unravel. There are sufficient documents and training to ensure that the system doesn't regress, and the next generation of managers can replicate the progress made thus far.
- Level 4: Quantitatively managed. The short answer here is that the organization is so good at whatever it's maturing that it is in a position to export its expertise to other organizations.
- Level 5: Optimizing. Nobody really ever gets here. Level 5 is where you're so darn good at what you're doing that you routinely produce groundbreaking solutions to long-standing problems. If you were an NFL team, you would be the Dallas Cowboys (who have been to a record number of Super Bowls, and won three of these championships from 1991–1995.)

The capability maturity model is a gorgeous piece of work. Once it was published, it didn't take long for other industries to recognize that they too went through a process structure very similar to the CMM©, and many sought to adapt this model to their industries. So, when PMI's College of Performance Management (CPM) first approached me to develop their Implementation Track, I naturally turned to the SEI CMM©. As I was conducting my initial research, I used a book by Kim Caputo (1991) entitled *CMM Implementation Guide, Choreographing Software Process Improvement*. Although the book-long metaphor of ballet dancing is highly irksome, this book did have valuable insights. Ms. Caputo reviewed the characteristics of the capability maturity model and examined more precisely the subject of implementation. Here's my paraphrase of what she asserted—that, in-between each CMM© Level, there are six steps:

1. Introduce an awareness of the capability you want to advance.
2. Scope it out, so that all who are directly participating understand what's expected of them.
3. Define the effort you intend to pursue.
4. Launch a pilot project and bring it in successfully.
5. Widespread group assimilation.
6. Institutionalization.

I'm going to submit a modified set of interlevel actions for PMOs in particular:

1. Introduce the project management capability that you are pursuing. Sell its attributes to superiors, and stress its ease of use to participants (more on this later).
2. Clearly define the scope of the implementation project, so that participants will know exactly what will be expected of them, and consumers of the information will not ask for more than you can provide (at least early on).
3. Identify those projects that will be initially contained in the project management information systems you will be introducing, and set about capturing the necessary data.
4. With the major or high-profile projects being reported, expand the system so that all of the project work within the organization is having its cost and schedule performance reported via your system and only your system.
5. Once the entire project portfolio has been captured, establish the project management way of doing things as standard throughout all levels of the organization.
6. Conduct an audit to see if you have attained the next level or phase depending on the business model being used.

Now, should the capability advancement agent undertake these tactics in the order stated, he would quickly come to the realization that the first three are pretty doable, but getting the fourth tactic finished is extremely difficult. This is known as the "Chasm of Adoption," (Caputo 1991, page 56,) where a singular lack of cooperation, known as the "silent veto," would disrupt the advancement of the capability. The silent veto, also known as the "slow roll" (more on this later), occurs when parts of the organization agree to participate with the advancement of the capability, but just don't show up when it's time for them to actually contribute. My interpretation of Ms. Caputo's solution to overcoming the silent veto is to go pedal-to-the-metal on enhancing communications. Get those people whom you believe are exercising the silent veto into a room and draw them out. Discover their concerns and misgivings, and convince them that they are mistaken in holding them. Other solutions to the slow roll include marginalizing those who attempt to engage in it or engaging in one of the tactics from Part 1 of this book. In my opinion, none of these solutions work. I've already written the reasons the tactics from Part 1 don't work and, while I'm aware that many problems are caused by a lack of communication, I believe that the majority are not. In the case of implementing project management techniques, my belief is that those opposed are, for the most part, perfectly clear on the project management advocates' intentions—they simply disagree and will engage in the silent veto or slow roll tactics until it becomes unviable for them. At that point, some will agree to participate, but others will certainly engage in more active opposition. In short, enhancing communications is not, in my opinion, the answer to overcoming the silent veto, the main obstacle in the path of maturing a process. Here, in my opinion, was the critical failure of the capability maturity model (CMM©). While the CMM© could note the structure of process improvement, and even provide a scorecard for assessing where the organization stood in regards to its progress, the CMM© itself could not help in driving an implementation. The PMO director who sought answers solely from the SEI CMM© was going to be frustrated. So, the question remained: how does one implement the capability of performing project management techniques in an organization where they are not universally employed?

Chapter Summary

There are boatloads of business models available for helping to lend structure to implementation efforts. While the capability maturity model provides a nifty gradation structure for furthering a given capability within the macro-organization, current writings on the subject fail to satisfactorily address a critical component: How to actually further a capability?

CHAPTER 9

Post's Theory

Yeah, but he's *our* zealot!

> —Dave Post, responding to a manager who complained that I was
> "too much of an earned value zealot."

The invaluable David Post, as of this writing an executive with Holmes and Narver, happened to be my boss at the time I was struggling with this particular issue. He had extensive experience in both project and facility management, with a very impressive resume. Dave would often come to my office at the end of the business day, and we would talk about project management and implementation theory, and the discussions became highly involved and intricate. Once, after having discussed the various structures and models available, Dave asserted an approach which I found to be highly intriguing. He drew a figure on my white board that looked like Figure 9-1.

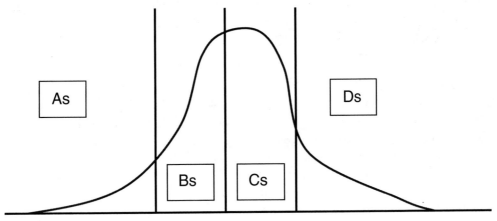

Figure 9-1.   Dave Post's drawing.

He explained the Figure 9-1 in the following way: The population represented in the bell curve are the members of the organization.

- The "As" are those who embrace change naturally. They're the ones who went out and bought Betamax format VHS machines. They will be willing participants in project management or any other implementation.
- The "Bs" are those in the organization who will cooperate, but must be shown how the new capability will help them personally, or, at least, their home organizations. They constitute a larger percentage of the overall organization, but they, plus the A's, do not create a usable majority.
- The "Cs" are those who will either "silent veto" you or else actively oppose your implementation agenda. They can only be won over by the coercive strategies.
- The "Ds" are those who will actively oppose your implementation, even in the face of the coercive strategies. They will never be won over and must be either marginalized or out-and-out eliminated from the organization in order for an implementation to go forward.

(To be precise, I'm pretty sure Dave didn't invent this approach by himself. Representing an organization as a traditional bell curve, and dividing it into types is somewhat common. Similar figures appear in the book *Crossing the Chasm* by Geoffrey A. Moore, HarperBusiness, 1991, as well as *CMM Implementation Guide*. But as far as I know the remainder of our discussion was based on his original research and experience.)

Dave then noted Step No. 3 of Ms. Caputo's approach: launch a pilot project. Dave theorized that, if the "pilot project" happened to be big enough, then all of those who belong to that project will be converted into the "B" classification of employees willing to participate in advancing project management techniques. If the silent veto strikes the macroorganization, the answer would be to reintroduce the capability, rescope its requirements, and then select another large project as the next pilot. With two or three large projects brought into the project management fold, most of the macro-organization would be participating anyway, and the tipping point for widespread group assimilation, if not already attained, would be very close. At the time Dave made his argument, I thought it very attractive. Even in retrospect, I would hardly be surprised if many a successful implementation was carried out in this way.

But I did have my objections.

The Problems with Post's Theory

The central problem with Post's theory is that, after having encountered the silent veto and being forced to return to the first step of the interlevel process, there is a limited number of times that the organization will tolerate a reintroduction (Caputo 1991). Potential participants simply become tired of listening to the particulars of another management initiative and tend to tune out. My take was that if the sought-after tipping point had not been attained before the organization would simply no longer listen when another maturation attempt was undertaken, then all that had gone before would unravel. And, when *that* occurred, then the organization would be left in worse shape than before the initial maturation effort had begun. The frustration factor would actually move the bell curve's lines of demarcation towards the left, making nominal resistors (Cs) out of nominal cooperators (Bs). Even with my objections, I had no viable alternative. Post's theory seemed to be the only viable option to overcoming the silent veto. Then, one day as I was driving to work, the solution hit me like an anvil from heaven.

The Solution

The Prisoner's Dilemma is considered the standard model for evaluating cooperation and defection among nonrelated biological units in a common environment. The story goes that you are a prisoner, and your jailer has come to you and offered to reduce your sentence if you inform on your cellmate. The dilemma comes about because you know your cellmate will receive the same offer. There are variations of the amount of time needed to serve for each decision scenario, but I will use the following four possible outcomes:

1. You inform on your cellmate, but he does not inform on you. This will result in your cellmate receiving 18 years sentence, and you walk free.
2. Conversely, if you do not inform on your cellmate, but he informs on you, he walks, and you receive 18 years. This outcome is known as the "sucker's payoff."
3. If neither of you informs on the other, you both receive 11 months.
4. If you both inform on the other, you both receive 5 years.

Here it is in table format:

	You Cooperate	**You Defect**
Cellmate Cooperates	Both receive 11 months	You walk, and your cellmate gets 18 years
Cellmate Defects	Cellmate walks, you receive 18 years ("Sucker's Payoff")	You both receive 5 years

In playing the Prisoner's Dilemma, conventional wisdom had held that you always inform on your cellmate in order to avoid being on the receiving end of the "sucker's payoff."

In 1981, Professor Robert Axelrod hosted an international competition between competing computer programs playing 200 iterations of the Prisoner's Dilemma to see if a consistently winning strategy would emerge (Axelrod 1984). The competing programs approached the problem from a wide variety of angles. Some, in keeping with conventional wisdom, informed every time. Others informed every other time, some the first 50 but not the remaining 150 iterations, and so forth. One program submitted by Anatol Rapoport won the overall competition by a healthy margin. It was named "Tit for Tat," and here's how it worked. The first iteration, it did not inform on its rival. Thereafter, it did whatever the other program did in the previous iteration.

After Tit for Tat had won the overall competition, some analysts sought to find out why. They developed some variances of Tit for Tat, one that informed the first time, and then did whatever the other program did in the previous iteration. Another variant did not inform the first five times, and then did the Tit for Tat approach. The variants always lost to the original, leading these analysts to assert that Tit for Tat's success was due to three factors:

1. It was initially "nice," in that it did not defect.
2. It punished immediately for defection.
3. It forgave immediately and completely for cooperation.

Meanwhile, back in my car on my way to work, I was becoming more and more excited as I realized that I may have found the missing link to furthering an implementation in the face of silent vetoes and slow rolls. After all, the primary difficulty in any kind of an implementation of this nature is securing cooperation within the macroorganization, and the Prisoner's Dilemma experiment appeared to yield a usable solution. The fact that, to a lesser extent, the Prisoner's Dilemma competition involved computer programs made it fit even better, since the key element to implementing project management lies within the establishment and use of cost and schedule performance measurement information streams, which are virtually always computer programs.

Yes, But Does The Solution Actually Work?

Based on the Tit for Tat solution of the Prisoner's Dilemma and the structure provided by the Capability Maturity Model©, I put together a specific set of actions to be used in implementing project management within the macro-organization (discussed later). But I had to find out if it worked.

In 2001, Dave Post and I rolled out this approach as the centerpiece for the College of Performance Management's (CPM-600) track, Implementation. The attendees in Tyson's Corner, VA, were highly supportive of the ideas, as reflected in their speaker assessment forms. With some scholastic confirmation under my belt, I was ready to try it out in a real PMO. Its first real-world test came in an organization responsible for US$40 million in project work, but did not have a portfolio-wide cost or schedule performance measurement system. They had made several attempts at implementing project management techniques and information systems, using many of the approaches that I have derided in earlier chapters. By the time this monster was dropped into my lap, any of the good will that may have existed for accepting such initiatives had largely evaporated. In a nominally hostile environment, I needed to produce results and fast.

This is how I did it. First, in keeping with the management information system axiom that you always begin with the end in mind, I went to the highest-level decision makers within the organization with a suite of cost and schedule performance reports. The formats ranged from Gantt charts and cost performance reports in format 1, all the way to the most intuitive formats, colorful and graphic, but able to convey summary project performance information quickly and accurately. Furthermore, I got them to agree to use their chosen formats as the basis for their monthly performance review meetings, which would prove to be key. Once the higher-ups selected their favorite formats, I knew how the end-state appeared.

Next, I engaged the first lesson from Tit for Tat—the new system had to be "initially nice." I interpreted that to mean that the new system had to be falling-off-a-log easy to install and use. The format that the executives had chosen was a chart indicating the cumulative cost and schedule performance indices in an XY chart that also showed the projects' relative sizes. Commonly known as a bubble chart, we nicknamed it the bull's-eye chart.

As a backup, we could also show the trends of the cost performance index and the schedule performance index, as shown in Figure 9-3.

Now, I'm fully aware of the data elements that most earned value management system supporters expect as part of their EVMS, being certified as an Earned Value Professional myself. But if you take an unflinching look at exactly what is the minimum data set required to produce a CPI/SPI chart, the answer is remarkably simple. You only need the following:

- A time-phased budget for the work, by WBS level,
- Actual costs, by month, and
- An estimate of the percent complete as of the end of the month.

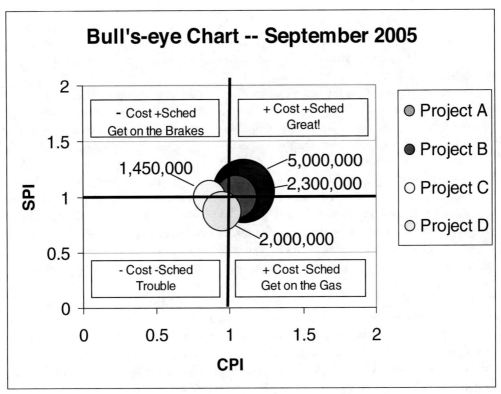

Figure 9-2.   Sample bull's-eye chart.

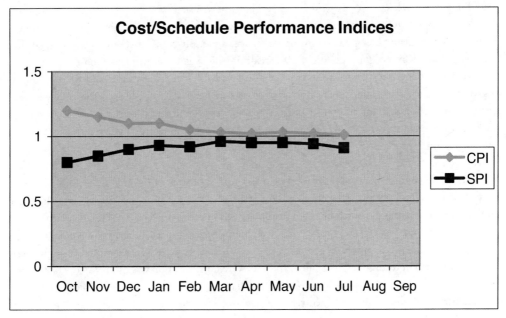

Figure 9-3.   Sample CPI/SPI chart.

And that's really all. The beauty of this *"de minimus"* approach is that, in almost all instances, the first two points are already in place via the organization's general ledger. The only additional data element we sought was an estimate of the projects' percent complete as of the end of each accounting period, which was monthly.

I took the opportunity to introduce the new system at the next manager's meeting. I showed everyone the new reports, and informed them that these were the report formats that were going to be used in the performance analysis meetings. Since the next step, that of describing exactly what was expected from each participant was so easy, I went ahead and told them that the only additional piece of information we would be gleaning from them was the percent-complete data. Their time-phased budgets and actual costs data elements were already being collected by the accountants. We took the next few weeks to collect our data elements, and set up a rudimentary CPI/SPI chart generator in Microsoft® Excel. At the end of the month, we collected what data we could and prepared the slides for the next performance analysis meeting.

At that meeting, some amazing things happened. When we projected the slides that contained the multiproject data, sorted by project type, the owning managers immediately began to discuss their performance in project management terms. Those projects that did not provide us even the minimum data set were listed in a text box off to the side of the reports. The organization's executives—the ones who had selected that particular format—asked those projects' representatives why their project was not included in the reports. Some attempted to claim that the data was too difficult to produce, at which they were roundly scorned for the utter idiocy of their statements. Others simply apologized for being late, and promised to meet the deadlines the next time around. By noting who had not participated in the system, we were executing Tit for Tat's second rule— respond immediately for any defection.

At the next month's meeting, the did-not-respond text box was empty. We had implemented a basic EVMS, moving a US$40 million organization from CMM© Level 1 to Level 2 in an astonishing seven weeks.

We were not quite through, however. In short order, we began to receive percent-complete figures that were clearly being gamed. In one instance, a percent-complete figure was provided that was computed to four significant digits. We realized this was done to yield a cost performance index of 1.0000, a clearly absurd number. We also recalled Tit for Tat's third and final lesson, to forgive completely and immediately once defectors had become cooperators. After all, we were seeking cooperation first and foremost, and the proper way to estimate percent complete on project work could be taught, while cooperation couldn't. A few tactfully worded conversations later, we were capturing legitimate cost and schedule information for the entire portfolio. The *de minimus* EVMS approach had worked, faster and better than anyone—even I—could have anticipated.

I would encounter many more successes using this approach, including a portfolio that was worth US$1.3 billion per year (yes, that's billion, with a "b"). Each time the scenario was chillingly similar: large programmatic portfolio, with insufficient or non-existing cost or schedule performance systems, where upper management was concerned about a programmatic disaster going unrecognized until it was too late to do anything about it . . . and someone had already attempted to implement project management techniques, had failed, and the overall organization was tired of being harangued on the subject. And in each case, a *de minimus* EVMS had captured the cost and schedule performance of the entire portfolio, with a markedly higher level of accuracy and timeliness than any system that had gone before, in such a short period of time as to inspire incredulity, even from those who had seen it occur first-hand.

Yes, the *de minimus* EVMS solution works, every time it's tried. It's not a magic bullet, though it is as close to one as exists in the project management implementation world. But it does, without a doubt, maximize the odds of success.

Chapter Summary

Dave Post's ideas for completing the capability maturity model were profound and insightful, but even he was missing one last, key component: maximizing the odds of macro-organization participation in the rollout of the PMO. That missing piece, provided by the analysis of the prisoner's dilemma and the competition to solve it, can be translated into a winning technical approach for implementing project management and conducting the affairs of the PMO. Adherence to this technical approach has proven to be successful multiple times in difficult circumstances, and can be expected to work every time it's tried.

CHAPTER 10

De Minimus EVMS Rollout

Numquam ponenda est pluralitas sine necessitate. (Do not assume more variables than neccessary.)

—William of Occam ("Occam's Razor")

There are two basic methodologies used for assessing project performance: earned value and critical path. But, while critical path is, well, critical to successfully managing a schedule, it can't provide information on cost performance. Earned value not only provides essential information on cost performance but also generates usable schedule performance data as well. Naturally, the optimal information stream includes both of these methodologies; but in an business environment where the PMO director is attempting to advance past CMM© Level 1, it's going to be necessary to select one of the methods as primary, and that method is earned value.

The basic earned value management system is the vehicle for advancing project management within the organization. But what's the driver? Where will we get the energy to actually move the organization in the right direction?

Anthony Robbins said "All personal breakthroughs begin with a change in beliefs. So, how do we change? The most effective way is to get your brain to associate massive pain to the old belief." This idea, writ large, means that the macroorganization will only change when it's in a state of pain. It has been my experience that, when the organization's top decision makers are given an opportunity to articulate exactly what it is that keeps them up at night, it is the fear that they are sitting on top of a project train wreck, and nobody is telling them about it. They hear about performance issues in projects only after it is too late to correct, and certainly too late to correct easily. Their frustration grows as they come to the realization that the problems that put millions of dollars and weeks of schedule at risk could have been readily and simply corrected, if only they had been communicated at the time they first manifest. It is this fear—this organizational pain—that serves as the energy driving the maturation of project management within the macr-oorganization. Here's how to use an EVMS to harness this energy.

Professor David Christensen of Southern Utah University once wrote an article on the stability of the cost performance index (CPI) (please refer to Appendix A for an earned value management system primer). For those of you who don't know, the CPI is a performance indicator generated by an earned value management system. It's calculated like this:

$$CPI = (BAC * \% \ Complete) \ / \ ACWP$$

where BAC is the project's budget at completion, and ACWP is the cumulative actual project costs. The BAC multiplied by the percent complete is another way of stating the earned value amount, so you're essentially dividing the earned value by the cumulative actual costs. Christensen's article evaluated hundreds of projects executed for the United States DOD and discovered something interesting: the CPI almost never varied more than 10 percentage points once the project had cleared the 15% complete point.

Okay, so why is this of importance to anyone outside the geek world of earned value practitioners? Because of a very common method for calculating a project's cost at completion. By dividing the CPI into the project's total budget, the result is a good estimate of how much a project will cost when it's done. How good? Well, based on Christensen's work, *it's accurate to within 10%!* By comparison, a professional estimator working with off-the-shelf estimating software and generating a detailed estimate that is so complete that it can be used to order personnel and material, is only accurate to within 15%. A simple EVMS is not only more accurate, but it is infinitely simpler, easier, faster, and cheaper to generate.

So, let's get back to tapping the executive's angst in order to drive project management maturity. The organization's highest decision makers are worried about projects being driven off of the tracks, resulting in millions of dollars in overruns and want an early warning system when one of them is in trouble. Even a very simple EVMS can fulfill this information need, and in a variety of formats, some so intuitive that even the highest level executives can immediately grasp what's being communicated. Add to this the fact that an EVMS can do so better than any of the competing information streams (more on competing systems later), and the PMO is in perfect position to use an EVMS to harness the organization's fear and pain in order to advance project management capabilities. All you have to do is to get into the hands of these angst-ridden executives a report that shows them which parts of their portfolios are in good shape, and which ones are on a course to overrun, and by how much. My favorite format for this is a histogram that lists projects from left to right in order of largest forecast overrun to largest forecast underrun, as in Figure 10.1.

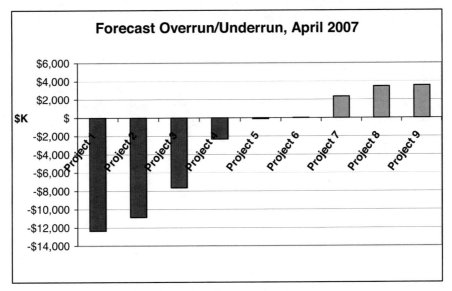

Figure 10-1.   Forecast overrun/underrun chart.

It doesn't take a project management aficionado to instantly recognize the extremely powerful nature of the information in this report. Many other intuitive and prescient reports are possible. When you are setting up your meeting with the organization's execs to discuss how you intend to implement project management, take along examples of these formats, and allow the decision-makers to select their favorite. Once they have done so, you have your deliverable from the basic EVMS. From now on, it's simply a matter of delivering it.

As you roll out your EVMS, remember the three lessons from Tit for Tat:

- The system has to be made to be extremely simple for participants.
- There must be a mechanism for responding to projects that attempt to opt out.
- All participants are golden, even if their data is suspect. Better data can be taught—participation can't.

In regards to the first aspect, to keep the EVMS simple, assess the bare essentials for keeping your reports flowing. This *de minimus* approach to earned value is truly effective, but it will have its detractors (more on that in Part 3). I have found that there are really only three data elements required for generating the entire suite of earned value reports:

- A time-phased budget at the reporting level of the WBS,
- Actual costs at the reporting level of the WBS, and
- An estimate of the percent that the work is complete at the reporting level of the WBS.

Even in organizations that are completely new to project management, the first two of these data elements are usually already in place because of the data needed by the general ledger. The lucky PMO director can easily find himself in a position to relieve the organization's executives' pain with nothing more than the collection of percent complete data. But even without such luck, the three data elements are remarkably simple to generate and collect. With these three data elements from all project work within the organization, it is possible to create and maintain the performance information streams that allow informed management of the organization. Once you have demonstrated this ability to spin data hay into information gold, the road ahead becomes, ironically enough, fraught with hazards.

Chapter Summary

An earned value management system, even a very simple one, represents an extremely powerful information stream. For a relatively small expenditure in collecting data, the resultant information provides strong returns and can serve as the primary driver in advancing the technical agenda of the PMO.

CHAPTER **11**

Maintaining the Centerpiece

Knowledge is a weapon. I intend to be formidably armed.

—Terry Goodkind's *The Sword of Truth*

A functioning earned value management system is an exceptionally powerful tool, even in its simplest forms. Remember the saying "Success has many fathers, but failure is an orphan?" In the world of competing information streams, it is self-evident that those who control essential management information streams wield significant amounts of organizational influence and power, and significant amounts of organizational influence and power are highly coveted. I will be addressing the dangers introduced by politics and rival systems in later chapters—for now, I'll address the resistance you should anticipate coming from within the ranks of project management practitioners.

The Great Estimate at Completion Debate

Of the many pieces of wrong-headed conventional wisdom floating around the project management world, the concept of a "bottom-up" estimate at completion (EAC) has to be among the most pernicious. This is the practice of re-estimating a project's remaining work, adding this figure to the cumulative actual costs and proclaiming that this amount is the most likely total cost at project completion. Not only is this way of generating the EAC inherently inaccurate (see Chapter 9), it creates a set of additional problems, to wit:

- We're re-estimating, right? What happens to the currently approved baseline? If it goes away, the project is operating off of an unapproved baseline. But if the new estimate is considered more accurate than the existing baseline, then the smartest move would be to manage off of the new estimate. But if you do *that*, then you're using two sets of books, which is blatant fraud.
- The only subjective part of a calculated EAC is the percent complete figure. However, a bottom-up estimate has hundreds, if not thousands, of subjective data elements. Since when is the approach with the maximum amount of subjectivity considered the best?
- It never fails: projects that routinely perform bottoms-up estimates will show zero (zero!) variance at completion until the project manager can simply no longer hide his issues from upper management. At that point, the lowest plausible variance is finally admitted to, which feeds the executives' fears to the maximum extent possible. After all, their biggest fear is that

they are sitting atop a project disaster, and no one will tell them about it. The main vehicle for these lies is the bottom-up EAC.

- Because the bottom-up EAC is inaccurate and, indeed, often used as a tool of deception, it paints all project management information systems with a broad brush of worthlessness. When the new PMO director attempts to sell the idea that an EVMS can foretell the project's cost future with a high degree of accuracy, those executives who have been subjected to the bottom-up approach will retain a high degree of skepticism, perhaps dooming your efforts before they even have an opportunity to prove themselves.

Unfortunately, the practice of generating an EAC with the bottom-up approach is ingrained in many projects and organizations, even ones that pride themselves on doing project management appropriately. Even when confronted with the facts surrounding the bottom-up approach's deficiencies, it has been my experience that its supporters will not back down. I have, however, discovered two tactics for resisting those who insist on performing bottom-up estimates. If you are being compelled to present a bottom-up EAC on your reports, consider doing the following:

- Allow the presentation of the bottom-up EAC, but also submit a calculated EAC from the earned value system. The difference between the two EACs will invariably generate questions during project reviews. In the long-term, it will become apparent which of the two methods for EAC generation is more accurate, and that will become the more coveted information item.
- If you must present the bottom-up EAC and are specifically precluded from showing a calculated EAC, find a way to present the to-complete performance index (TCPI) figure as well (complete EVMS formulae are shown in Appendix A). The TCPI is an indicator of how well the project must perform in order to achieve a set target, in this case, the bogus EAC. Recall from Dave Christensen's work that a CPI almost never changes more than 10 percentage points in either direction once the project has cleared the 15% point. The explanations that project managers can attempt to give to show how their current cost performance index of 0.87 will suddenly morph into a TCPI of 1.21 can become hilarious.

My Mom Always Said That No Girl Was Good Enough For Her Baby

She really did. My wife was a good sport for a long time about this sentiment, even though it was obviously false. Similarly, the second most common and most powerful opposition to the introduction of a simple EVMS will come from those within the project management world who will insist that any simple system is not good enough. They will ferociously maintain that the system's output is worthless unless:

- You have a resource-loaded schedule in a critical path-capable software package.
- The methods for assessing percent complete are consistent with the ANSI standard for earned value (748).
- The basis of estimate (BOE) for all work is demonstrably accurate.
- All 42 C/SCSC criteria are religiously followed.
- Desktop instructions and other documents have been created and approved.
- All work is captured in work packages, with the appropriate signatures.
- The system is done their way, and no other.

If ever the axiom "excellence is the enemy of good enough" was appropriate to a situation, the introduction of a simple EVMS is it. Whether they realize it or not, these people are maximizing your threat profile from those who sponsor rival systems, or those people who simply want (or need) to see your efforts fail. Yet, under the guise of wanting nothing more than to improve the quality of the information being presented to the executives, their objections often get a good deal of traction, and can result in a large amount of damage to your efforts.

The "BOE has to be perfect" argument is the easiest to refute. Earned value analysis has a degree of self-correcting capacity inherently present, which negates the need for perfect planning—as if perfect planning ever has or ever will exist. Consider the example of a project that was originally estimated for US$100,000, but, had the estimator been omniprescient, the estimate would have been US$200,000. At the 25% complete point, though, the EVMS shows that, while they are 25% done, they have actually spent US$50,000. The calculated EAC would immediately indicate that the final cost will be US$200,000 (at that rate of performance). Clearly, a perfect estimate is not required for a simple EVMS to generate the correct answer.

All remaining arguments along the lines of your simple EVMS not being "good enough" can be thwarted—ironically, with the graded approach counter. I think that the entire graded approach to implementing project management is as intellectually vacuous as alchemy (more on this later), but it is so ingrained in many organizations that it can be used to refute the not-good-enough-fast-enough crowd effectively.

As you roll out your nascent EVMS, clearly articulate your intentions to your staff (see Chapter 6). Make sure they understand that, while you will be happy to hear their concerns about information quality, they are not to bad-mouth the new system in front of customers or rivals. Be prepared to release or reassign those on your team who are unwilling to comply.

Manage your customers' expectations. Once they have selected a format to receive their cost and schedule performance data, resist their requests to enhance beyond your ability to provide. Deliver your reports, respond when projects attempt to opt out, and treat as royalty all who participate, no matter how bad their data looks. The *de minimus* EVMS is the centerpiece of your implementation, harvesting as it has the fear and pain within the organization that will drive the organization to change. Address internal challenges as I have laid out here and prepare for the exterior barriers that will be presenting themselves.

Chapter Summary

Even nominal supporters of earned value management systems can detract from your efforts, due to the adoption of extraneous practices associated with EVMSs. Maintaining the veracity of the basic system, while deterring those who would embrace the basic system's rivals, is essential to the ultimate success of the PMO.

References

Axelrod, R. 1984. *The evolution of cooperation.* New York: Basic Books.

Caputo, K. 1991. *CMM® implementation guide: Choreographing software process improvement.* Boston: Addison Wesley Professional.

Moore, G., 1991, *Crossing the Chasm,* HarperBusiness

Christensen, D. S., & Heise, S. (1993, Spring). Cost performance index stability. *National Contract Management Journal, 25:* 7–15.

PART 3

Hazards along the Way

O villain, villain, smiling, damned villain!
My tables—meet it is I set it down
That one may smile, and smile, and be a villain:
At least I'm sure it may be so in Denmark.

—Hamlet, Act 1, Scene 5

The previous parts of this book have been aimed at selecting the best possible technical approach to implementing your project management systems or advancing your organization's project management maturity. In many ways, that's the easy part since attempts to adopt and adapt specific technical agendas to achieve a desired end can be to some degree quantified, classified, and observed to be successful or not. It's as close as we project management types will get to the scientific approach—watch an idea be presented, pressed forward, and succeed or fail, like so many experiments being performed on the members of the organization, just without the white lab coats and clipboards. But this part of the book will touch on Hamlet's frustration, that of human duplicity utterly derailing the higher purpose being pursued. We'll start with that favorite cause of undetermined PMO failure, "politics."

CHAPTER 12

Politics

Politics is the art of looking for trouble, finding it whether it exists or not, diagnosing it incorrectly, and applying the wrong remedy.

—Ernest Benn

Every manager and team member is aware of the potential destructive capabilities of office politics, but few know how to manage it. For the sake of discussion, I will define politics in the office as "that energy spent pursuing a personal agenda that is incompatible with the macro-organization's stated technical agenda."

By this definition, a junior team member befriending an executive is not political; but, if that friendship results in that team member's ideas getting furthered at the expense of superior concepts, it becomes political at that point. The reason an organization with a highly politically charged environment is more likely to fail is because the best ideas, approaches, and solutions have a lesser chance of being recognized, much less pursued. Human nature being what it is, even in those organizations that can make the most legitimate claims to being meritocracies, the best ideas presented by slovenly employees will not attain the same traction as goofy ideas put forth by attractive personnel. That's life in the cubical farm, but these environmental parameters can be recognized and addressed.

Some managers will attempt to control the ebb and flow of political power by controlling the lines of communications. An example would be a middle manager becoming incensed with a subordinate making a pitch to the middle manager's superior. But any attempt to control these lines of communications will prove futile. Whether it's over the water cooler, in the break room, or at the company picnic, it's impossible to manage or control who communicates with whom within the macroorganization and attempts to interfere will make the would-be controller appear petty or, well, controlling.

Political agendas can only be pursued as long as they are not exposed. The moment that a course of action is recognized as benefiting a few at the expense of the macro-organization, it is doomed. Our friends, the accountants, have had a great deal of success in asserting that the calculation for determining the return on investment (ROI) is some kind of litmus test for evaluating whether or not any proposed course of action is good for the organization. By extension, pursuit of anything with a negative ROI must be purely political, right? But, as discussed in an earlier chapter, their techniques, ROI included, are designed to assess the performance of assets, not project work. Besides, as Tom Peters has pointed out in dramatic fashion, there are many acts which may have been evaluated as having a positive ROI, but are actually disastrous for the organization. The converse is true, particularly in the realm of project management, that acts which cannot be evaluated with regards to the ROI at all, or positively, may actually be of great benefit.

About That Smiling . . .

You are going to encounter people within your organization who wish for your attempts to further project management to fail. That's pat. In fact, the organization can be broken out into Post-like categories along the lines of whether or not they want you to succeed, and how they are willing to present themselves. Think of them as falling into one of the following categories:

- They do want you to succeed and are willing to say so. These are allies, and they're pure gold.
- They do want you to succeed, but are unwilling to advertise this fact. These are passive supporters. You can't call on them for help in your implementation, but at least they're not opposing you.
- They do not want you to succeed and are willing to say so. Honest, intellectual debate is okay, especially since project management supporters happen to occupy the intellectual high ground. They may or may not come around, but at least you know where they're coming from.
- As said in the classic 1960s American television series *Lost in Space,* "Danger, Will Robinson, Danger!" This last category is pure poison. They do not want you to succeed, and they will either not say so, or, even worse, they will present as if they do want you to prevail.

The former subcategory of bullet #4—those who want you to fail, but are unwilling to articulate as such—will invariably employ the silent veto tactic to prevent your PMO from succeeding. Ms. Caputo's recommended approach of enhancing communications lines to overcome their resistance is futile for this reason. These people do not suffer from a lack of communication. They are active opponents of your implementation. The response tactic in the recommended technical approach is designed to simply out their opposition. Recall the previous paragraph's assertion that a demonstrably political act cannot survive being identified as such. By responding to the silent veto-ers as they attempt to opt-out, you remove the power from their tactic. They simply can't opt out without showing themselves to be contrary to the macro-organization's goals.

But the second subcategory of bullet four—those who oppose your efforts, but present as if they want you to succeed—these are the puff adders situated on your path to PMO success. And, if you believe they aren't there, think again. From their vantage point of assumed golden allies, they can inflict fatal damage quickly, easily, and without exposing themselves to any kind of retribution. Usually this damage is inflicted during *ex parte* meetings they have with upper management, where they can lay their misbegotten charges against the PMO without fear of opposition or contradiction. From their perch of PMO ally, their assertions can go far with the flimsiest of cover, provided by the perception that these snakes are trying to help advance management capability.

Keep in mind also that these cobras can be inside the PMO, as well. I had the unfortunate experience of directing a large and demonstrably successful PMO that had one viper in my inner circle who connected with a coral snake in the organization's upper management. The results were swift, encompassing, and fatal.

As in the examples of other political maneuver-ers, your best hope is to reveal these people's real agenda. Expose them as opposers of your agenda, not supporters. While their communications and ex parte conversations with higher-ups cannot be controlled, you can try to make it clear that, in all matters pertaining to project management implementation, your voice is definitive and ought to be considered the final word on the subject. This places the vipers at the disadvantage of being clearly outside their appropriate arena whenever they spout their poison against you, your PMO, and your agenda. This tactic does not guarantee that their words won't have traction with the decision makers—it merely lessens the odds that they will prevail against you.

Unless you are a mongoose, you are not going to beat these people at their own game. Your favored tactic here is to draw them out of their snake dens, into the open light of evaluating competing technical visions. Your goal of furthering project management capability within your organization occupies the strategic high ground here. Their goals of furthering their careers by introducing substandard information streams (that they own, of course) as competition to yours are poisonous to the organization, and must be called out as such.

Chapter Summary

The PMO director will face political opposition. There's really no way of avoiding it. This opposition often proves fatal and is usually executed via ex parte conversations held among your detractors and the organization's decision makers at the highest levels. It's impossible to prevent such communications, so don't even try to control them. Your best bet is to establish that your PMO is the source and residence of all cost and schedule performance information, and that you are the sole decision maker in matters of implementation. From this perch it's possible to reveal the more politically charged agendas once they have been exposed as working against your verifiably beneficial approach to implementation.

CHAPTER 13

Rival Systems

Where facts are few, experts are many.

—Donald R. Gannon

The point of any management information system is to put usable information into the hands of the decision makers. In order to be usable, the information should have the following characteristics:

- *Accuracy:* Inaccurate information is worse than useless, it's actually misleading.
- *Timeliness:* Problems have the nasty habit of growing unless they are addressed. Late performance information invites such growth.
- *Completeness:* Part of the difficulty in being a manager is having to make decisions based on incomplete information, so deliberately leaving off some parts of the portfolio from participation in an information system is just plain goofy.

Earned value management systems are the very best at providing key elements of management information including:

- Forecasts of how much a project will cost at its completion.
- Forecasts of how much a project will cost at any future month.
- Identification of which activities are being executed efficiently and which aren't.
- Identification of which activities are being executed effectively and which aren't.
- Identification of which parts of the organization are performing better than others.

While the critical path method is superior for forecasting when a project and its activities will be completed, earned value does a fair job with that piece of information as well. Consider for a moment, the power inherent in having the information in the bullet points previously mentioned combined with the characteristics in the bullets in the previous paragraph. The manager who has command of this information can't help but be far, far more effective at attaining the organization's goals then those managers who don't. This kind of information will even help keep chronically inept managers from incurring project overruns and delays. Those people who generate and control this kind of information stream within the macro-organization wield considerable clout, which makes being that information generator extremely attractive to those who desire to wield considerable organizational clout. Unless those people who seek to gain organizational power by controlling key information streams happen to be on the team working the earned value management system, they will almost invariably present a rival, non-EVMS-based information system as the source and residence of cost and schedule performance data. Unfortunately, these supporters of rival systems are often successful in their attempts to elbow the EVMS proponents aside either because upper management is ignorant of EVMS capabilities or through the political machinations that accompany any illegitimate power grab. Learning how to recognize the inherent flaws in the rival systems and successfully marginalizing them, then, becomes absolutely essential to maintaining a successful project management office.

Budgets and Actuals

The main breeding ground of rival information systems comes from our good friends, the accountants. It's not that they're bad people with a quirky affection for suspenders; it's just that they've been taught things that aren't so. For example, I don't know if they've been taught this out loud, but, if you were to inject any of them with truth serum, they would admit that they believe that the source and residence of any piece of management information that contains a dollar sign should be the accounting system. Since most accountants I've met firmly believe that the accounting system should, for example, provide cost projections, they respond to earned value practitioners who make the (valid) claim that an EVMS is superior at projecting costs as interlopers.

The specific data items that the GAAP aficionados will assert are better handled by the general ledger are:

Information Element	Valid EVMS Approach	Flawed GAAP Approach
At-completion costs	Several, with BAC/CPI being the most common.	Several, but they're all wrong. Common ones include performing a regression analysis on actual costs curves or previous cumulative variances.
Cost performance	The earned value amount minus actual costs.	The budgeted amount minus actual costs.
Schedule performance	The earned value amount minus the budgeted amount.	The budgeted amount minus actual costs (it's the wrong answer to more than just one question).
Income projections	The sum of the portfolio's calculated variances at completion combined with the result of multiplying the proposal win rate by the cumulative proposal backlog.	The result of multiplying the current return on investment by the addition of current total assets and planned acquisitions. (I'm not making this up. That's really how they think.)

Organizational performance	Cross-hatching the activities' cost and schedule performance data by organization. This is usually done using a responsibility/ accountability matrix.	The budgeted amount minus actual costs, adjusted by organization ("when all you have is a hammer, everything looks like a nail").

Old myths die hard, and the hammerlock the accountants have on cost information streams isn't going to be overcome easily. In those instances where the information coming from your PMO is being challenged by the accountants, try to arrange for the earned value information to be evaluated on the same basis as the general ledger info. Do the accountants claim to have the better system for projecting at-completion costs? Let them prove it. A simple comparison is all you are seeking, because the eventual winner of this competition is pretty clear—the EVMS will provide the aforementioned information elements faster, cheaper, more comprehensively, and, perhaps most important, more accurately.

The notion that a cost variance is calculated by comparing budgeted costs to actual costs also dies hard. It's just so clear, isn't it? How are we doing against our budget? Just subtract one from the other, right? Some of the nastiest looks I have drawn from accountants follow the strongly asserted fact that comparing budgets to actual costs is useless. A cost variance is earned value minus actual costs, period. A schedule variance is the earned value figure minus the budget. That's how variances are computed, and anyone who attests differently is either lying or ignorant. Accountants fall into the previous category—they should know better—but engineers, scientists, lawyers, and other professions, buttressed in believing this myth by the accountants, need to be educated, lest they become actively engaged in opposing your EVMS implementation. Often this can be accomplished by inviting them to take a look at their "variance" of the difference between the budget and actual costs. If it's a negative number—does that mean that the project is overspent, or ahead of schedule? If it's a positive number—is the project being done efficiently, or slowly? It's impossible to say, without some quantification of the work performed.

Milestone Lists

Another primary source of rival systems comes from people who do not understand the basics of schedule management. You'll know these people because they consistently try to manage schedules with milestone lists and action item trackers. Recall the structure of all legitimate management information systems in Figure 13-1.

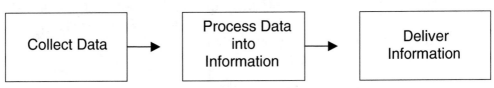

Figure 13-1.   Legitimate MIS structure.

Contrast Figure 13-1 with Figure 13-2 that depicts virtually all illegitimate management information systems:

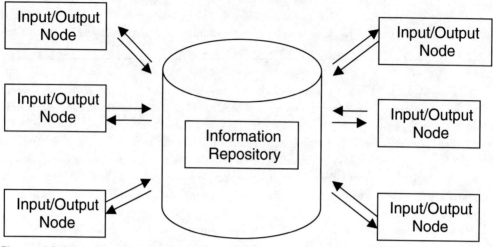

Figure 13-2.   Illegitimate MIS structure.

Action item trackers and milestone "management" systems almost always have this structure. Note that these systems do not employ data gathering and processing into information cycles. They are simply data repositories or polls. The problems with using polls as usable information are legion and include the following:

- Someone always has better or more recent information. If the data mined from a poll is contradicted by another source, how do you know which is accurate?
- Usable management information always seeks to minimize or eliminate the amount of purely subjective data in the system. Polls consist almost exclusively of subjective data.
- The so-called milestone tracking systems that do not employ critical path or percent-complete analysis are almost always comically inaccurate. These systems are composed of named milestones—their beginning dates, planned completion dates, and estimated completion dates. In every single such system I've observed, the planned and estimated completion dates are the same, until it's painfully obvious to everyone involved that the milestone will be missed.

As lame as these rival systems are, they, like their general ledger counterparts, are often aggressive competitors with legitimate systems, like earned value or critical path.

Ironically, milestone tracking systems and action item lists can be converted from the Dark Side into something useful, and the answer lies with—what else?—earned value. Recall the formula for computing a project's (or task's) cost at completion:

$$EAC = BAC / CPI$$

Where EAC is the estimate at completion, BAC is the budget at completion, and CPI is the cost performance index. Since the CPI is calculated from:

$$CPI = (\% \text{ Complete} \cdot BAC) / ACWP$$

where ACWP is the cumulative actual costs, the original estimate at completion formula can be simplified as:

$$ACWP / \% \text{ Complete}$$

Interestingly, this formula also works for duration! In other words if you want a fairly accurate estimate of when an activity will finish, divide its cumulative duration by an estimate of its percent complete. The beauty of this converted earned value formula is that when you seek to implement it, you can sell it as an enhancement to the (currently invalid) milestone or action item tracking system that is in place. Since the baseline start date, and therefore the cumulative duration data elements are already known, all the milestone/action item tracking system administrator needs is the percent-complete figure. Again, we see a scenario where most of the data elements needed for a basic earned value management system are in place, and all we need is one more: the estimated percent complete figure. The canny project management office director is now in a position to piggyback on those pushing their milestone/action item tracking system's desire for that last piece of data which will legitimize their systems to help bring a nascent EVMS into existence. When it comes to the spider-like data structure drivers, a win-win solution can be attained.

Risky Business

I used to be a big proponent of performing risk analysis on a project's baseline, as early in the cycle as the cost and schedule baselines could be accurately created. But I was also born and spent my youth in the Southern United States, where a common and valuable piece of wisdom was "don't borrow trouble." During the years my management style was developing, I wanted to incorporate this axiom into my approach, so I needed to be able to articulate it more precisely. I believe that this axiom can be paraphrased as "don't project negative consequences onto predicted scenarios where you don't have enough information to do a decent evaluation." When I developed this definition, I suddenly realized that anticipating future negative consequences to predicted scenarios was at the heart of worrying—and the essence of risk analysis.

Essentially, risk analysis is institutionalized worrying, writ large and resting on a foundation of statistical analysis methods (I have this sinking feeling that, should I pursue an elected office within PMI, my opponents will use this sentence as the pull-quote to assert that I'm blatantly unqualified. Ah, well, another promising career in politics down the tubes!). The future is notoriously difficult to predict, and cranking up the sophistication of statistical modeling can't change that fact. Why? The reason has to do with more management information system (MIS) theory. All MISs fall into one of two categories: feedback and feedforward. Feedback systems are the most common, and include the General Ledger, earned value, critical path, and the like. They quantify what has happened and use that data to make assertions about the present and, sometimes, the future. Since they deal with what has (verifiably, hopefully) already happened, their data is mostly, if not exclusively, objective. Feedforward systems, conversely, are oriented towards things that are projected to happen in the future. Not to be overly pedantic here, but things that are projected to happen in the future, by definition, cannot be objective. They MUST be subjective. Referencing figure 13-1, reflect on what truly reliable output can be derived when the whole of the data gathering phase is predicated on purely subjective data. And any system predicated wholly (or even mostly) on subjective data should always be suspect.

An unfortunate myth has crept into project management circles, that any time a project incurs delays, overruns, or quality problems that the proximate cause was a lack of planning. And yet, so prevalent is this myth that it has fueled a large industry devoted to analyzing things that might go wrong in a project's future, and quantifying them. But this raises the question: does such quantification really help anybody, or any thing? As I have stated previously, managers must make decisions based on incomplete information. Decisions based on complete information fall into the realm of engineers, and managers are never that lucky.

Project managers are going to tackle the problems before them, and they will take the best technical approach available at the time of project initiation. I don't want anybody to misunderstand me here: if a different technical approach should have been taken, and variance analysis data can inform the project manager to consider alternatives, great. But of what value is a risk manager who, Cassandra-like, warns the project manager of things that could go wrong with the selected technical approach? Don't project managers, almost by definition, spend more than enough time anticipating things that could go wrong as it is?

Upon further review, I came to the conclusion that the insistence on performing a risk analysis qualifies as a "slow roll" behavior. Apart from estimating the amount of cost or schedule contingency appropriate for a given baseline, performing a risk analysis brings nothing of value to the overall project management information system. Consider how a manager would become aware that an analyzed risk event had occurred. If it's because actual costs have exceeded the budget, then we're performing the invalid budgets vs. actuals "analysis." Otherwise, we're counting on the earned value management system to inform us which, of course, assumes the existence of the EVMS *before* the risk analysis system is in place. I'm aware that many project managers and/or their customers love to be able to say that their cost baseline "has a confidence level of X percent," but the accuracy of the original cost and schedule baseline is not a function of the subsequent risk analysis. Rather, it is a function of the method used in creating those estimates in the first place.

There currently exists many stand-alone and bolt-on risk analysis computer programs. I view all of them as rival systems. Why? Recall the necessity in delivering accurate and timely earned value information into the hands of the organization's decision makers. Risk analysis does not further this goal. Recall also the techniques employed in the "slow roll" behaviors, those of dissipating or wasting time and energy in pursuits that do not add to the immediate goals, and helping to slow the creation of usable baselines. Risk analysis does both. Essentially, the PMO director is well-advised to only perform risk analysis when it is required by the customer. In all other instances, you have better places to spend your time, energy, and organizational clout.

Chapter Summary

Since it is imperative that PMO personnel avoid loser tactics (Part 1) and execute a winning technical approach to furthering project management (Part 2), wasting time, effort, and money pursuing rival systems is potentially fatal to your PMO's success. Such rival systems, if not already in place, lie dormant, and you should anticipate that they will be furthered at the expense of your (valid) EVMS. Do not allow the rival systems analyzed in this chapter to elbow you and your team aside. Anyone pursuing a *de minimus* EVMS approach owns the MIS high ground outright, especially when it comes to cost and schedule information. Those pushing rival systems are charlatans or quacks, and should be considered as such.

CHAPTER 14

Frontal Assaults

The lion cannot protect himself from traps, and the fox cannot defend himself from wolves. One must therefore be a fox to recognize traps, and a lion to frighten wolves.

—Niccolo Machiavelli

A ctive, open, and energetic opposition to your PMO's goals is something of a rarity. The widespread acceptance and acknowledgement of the validity of project management techniques makes such opposition a risky proposition. But over-the-top resistance, which I'll call a frontal assault, does occur, and the PMO professional must be prepared to overcome it.

Think of resistance to project management implementation as coming from three potential sources:

- From within the PMO organization itself,
- From within the macroorganization, but outside the PMO, and
- From outside the organization.

Depending on the source of the resistance, the tactics used to slow (or even reverse) project management implementation can expect varying levels of success, unless you are there to stop them.

Resistance from within the PMO Itself

This type of resistance comes most often when a new director of the PMO has inherited the staff from a previous director, especially if the predecessor happened to be the one who created the team in the first place. Chances are the previous director failed, but the precise reasons for having failed are either unclear or have not been articulated to the PMO staff. This leaves them with the impression that it was some vague reason, such as "politics," or the well-known myth that changing the organizations' culture to be more accommodating of PM techniques takes boatloads of time, were to blame. The odds are good that a significant part of the PMO will view the new director with mistrust and apprehension.

Some of this can be overcome using the leadership tactics described in Chapter 6. By clearly articulating your technical agenda and expectations, you can win over those members of the PMO who are knowledgeable enough to recognize that your technical agenda will work. Others will need more persuasion. The remnant must be recognized early on and swiftly marginalized, both technically and in their relationships with the others in the PMO.

Occasionally those who require marginalizing will do you a favor and come right out in open opposition. I had one such fellow throw a tantrum in my office, so it was a relatively easy thing to go to his line manager and arrange for a swift reassignment. More common, however, are those who are perfectly content to sit in their offices and draw their paychecks while damaging your odds of success. Consider employing the following tactics to marginalize them:

- Give them the more unpleasant, less critical assignments. Putting together a portfolio-wide baseline involves lots of legwork. Since you set the technical agenda, and this stuff has to happen anyway . . .
- Formalize your communications with a written plan. The excellent Frederick Tarantino, currently head of the Universities Space Research Association, called this a "zipper plan," since the teeth in a zipper always line up with their counterparts. Make it clear and formal which parts of your organization are authorized to speak about which specific topics, and respond immediately when, say, the estimators attempt to communicate on behalf of the schedulers. This zipper plan will help minimize (but not eliminate) bad or incomplete communications from jeopardizing your efforts, and lessen the opportunities your in-house detractors have to do so.
- Be absolutely clear which employees are in your favor and which are not, based on the following classifications:
  - Technically competent employees who are cooperating with your agenda,
  - Less-than-competent employees who are cooperating with your agenda,
  - Technically competent employees who are opposing your agenda, and
  - Incompetent opposers.

Make the first category your "inner circle." Arrange for the next category to receive training, out of town, if possible, so it's more of a perk. Continue your efforts to convert the third category, but don't let them have the coveted assignments or offices. And finally, take advantage of the myriad, subtle ways that exist to show your mild disdain for the last group.

- Forbid all ex parte conversations from your team to you. Going to the boss and complaining about another member of the team is one of the most pernicious practices that can afflict a PMO. It is perhaps the leading generator of mistrust and infighting within a team. Make it clear to every member of the PMO that should any one employee approach you with a complaint about another team member, that that team member will be immediately brought into the discussion so as to present their side of the story.

As with the macro-organization, the characteristic you covet most is cooperation, and you should manage your team accordingly. By employing the bulleted tactics within your PMO organization, you are maximizing the odds of developing a cohesive, performing team in the shortest possible time.

Resistance from within the Organization, but Outside the PMO

Although addressed throughout the rest of this book, it's good to summarize the panzer attack paths from this, the most daunting of your PMO's opponents. Assuming that you are not pursuing any of the tactics from Part 1, and trying to implement the recommendations in Part 2, your primary opposition from outside your team but within the company will come in these forms:

- Rival systems from rival organizations, purporting to be able to feed decision-makers information as powerful as that generated by the earned value management system.
- Those who admit to the power of an EVMS, but attempt to paint it as too difficult or expensive to initiate or maintain.
- Those who will insist that the *de minimus* EVMS is generating poor or inaccurate information.
- The "expectation-setters," who will assert that any preferred management information system must be able to provide their favorite information tidbit, or else it's not valid, and therefore undeserving of upper management support.

Each of these sources of resistance is provably invalid, but that doesn't stop them from gaining traction in the organization's upper echelons. But it has been my experience that these sources of resistance are best overcome by the PMO focusing in on its primary mission: that of placing into the hands of decision makers the powerful information stream that is routinely generated from a functioning earned value management system. Focus in on that mission like a laser beam, and these sources of opposition will fall by the wayside. However, waste time, energy, and resources on pursuing the tactics that Part 1 shows don't work, and these sources of resistance have legs. Pursue the misguided techniques listed in Part 1 of this book, and you hand your detractors more than enough power to undercut your efforts and undo your PMO and, yes, it really is that simple.

Resistance from Outside your Organization

Resistance from outside the organization will come from two sources: the customer and the competition. While customers will almost never openly oppose the use of project management techniques, they can and will have some rather odd notions of how project management techniques should be manifested. A general rule is to never allow your customer to review or possess a copy of your detailed critical path schedule, since their "experts" will have unlimited latitude to fuss about your activities durations, schedule logic, basis of estimate—they can go on forever from just one 1000-activity status file. It's much, much safer to clearly lay out the reporting requirements in the project execution plan (PEP) and adhere to them religiously (WHAT? You don't have a PEP? Report yourself to the project management authorities immediately!).

More dangerous is your competition. If, either by reading this book first or by some miracle, they have advanced their organization's project management maturity level beyond yours, they are in a position to make the case that, since they are ahead of you in this critical capability, they should receive more business than your organization does. Particularly in the public arena, the customer tends to view contractors as devious and untrustworthy. The very best way of overcoming this lack of trust is to put into the customers' hands accurate and timely project performance information. The refusal (or inability) to do so simply adds to the customers' mistrust and angst, leading them to a point where they are willing to spend more money on a poorer performer, as long as the poorer performer is keeping them up-to-date on performance, and telling the truth. So the lack of project management maturity becomes a vulnerability, one that is easily exploited by those who not only want your PMO to fail, but also your entire organization to crash and burn.

"You cannot wake a man who is pretending to be asleep" goes the Chinese proverb. Similarly, it's hard to convince the organization that has a façade of performing project management techniques well to *really* do those techniques, for real, on real projects, and across entire portfolios.

The solution? Again, focus like a laser on producing timely, accurate, and *portfolio-wide* performance information, and make that information available (at the appropriate levels) to your customers. This act will engender trust, demonstrate your project management capabilities, and lower (or eliminate) the threat profile represented by competitors seeking to undermine your organization on the basis of lack of project management maturity.

Code Words and Trojan Horses

Of course, quickly and reliably identifying your opposition is key to being able to deal with them. Since one category of opposition is those who present as if they are your supporters but are, in fact, your detractors, quick and reliable identification is rarely easy. Consider the following:

- You have a limited amount of time and energy to enact your *de minimus* EVMS across the programmatic portfolio.
- Professor Baker's insight on the slow roll, and how those opposed to your technical agenda need not do so overtly. They can simply slow your progress, causing your energy to dissipate and time to expire before you can achieve success.
- Even renowned management authors, consultants, and professors can assert poorly thought-out ideas and concepts in nearly opaque verbiage, and some members of the organization will take such concepts as authoritative.

Now you have the ingredients for an implementation disaster.

Here, then, is a partial list of code words used by those who are trying to appear as if they want a successful project management implementation, but are actually working against it (whether they know it or not):

Code Word or Phrase	Why It's Invalid
Graded approach	See Chapter 7
Consistent with the *PMBOK® Guide*	The *PMBOK® Guide* is a collection of subject areas that some academics and professionals believed should be the basis for all project management expertise. It is not an implementation guide.
Need for procedures, guides, documentation	See Chapter 4
(Famous person) says you should . . .	See Chapter 5
Well, I'm a (insert degree or certification letters here), and I think . . .	I think you should see Chapter 2

We have to make sure the numbers coming out of the EVMS match the general ledger precisely.	Sure, if we can simultaneously ensure that the general ledger isn't attempting to generate figures it shouldn't, like cost performance, estimate at completion, schedule performance . . .
It takes time to change the culture . . .	The "culture change" crowd gives cover to those engaging in the slow-roll behaviors.
The earned value data is inaccurate.	Compared to what? It's far more accurate in matters of EAC calculation or cost performance than anything that the general ledger is capable of producing, or any other system or methodology, for that matter.
The earned value data is irrelevant.	This is another way of saying "nobody should expect me to report on project performance."
The baselines that serve as the basis for the EVMS aren't using the most recent rates.	EV has a self-correcting ability that does not require continual updates whenever labor or material rates change. Only the (illegitimate) practice of recalculating remaining work and adding that figure to cumulative actual costs requires the most recent rates (see Chapter 11).
I'm more familiar with the particulars of this project, and don't need an EVMS to report on at-completion costs.	This is another way of saying "My subjective opinion is more accurate than any objective performance reporting, and I dare you to state otherwise." Usually spoken by exceedingly arrogant and inept managers.

Sometimes the instances of the utterings of these code words goes beyond a momentary disagreement about the path forward you have selected for your PMO. It may actually be that your opponents are of like mind in their opposition to your technical agenda AND their approach to slowing or stopping it. I'm not necessarily talking about a conspiracy here either. Because so much of the conventional wisdom in advancing a project management capability within the organization is simply wrong-headed, your opposition may have actually come to similar conclusions by imbibing of the same conventional wisdom—sort of like a Jungian group-think or mob mentality. These Trojan horse ideas, which appear benign or even helpful, will work against the realization of a successful PMO and represent a real hazard to the furthering of project management capability.

For example, take two of the accountants' most common code phrases, the "EVMS data must match the general ledger" and "The cost baseline must have the most recent rates." Innocuous on their face, but taken together they further the flat-out wrong notion that the general ledger is the appropriate residence and source of all management information that has a dollar sign in front of it. But much like Cassandra was shouted down when she correctly identified the disaster that would result from bringing the real Trojan horse inside the city gates, the PMO director who calls the accounting manager on his managerial ploy Trojan horse can expect to receive derision from the higher-placed ignoramuses in the organization.

Another common Trojan horse is offered up by those who are trying to manage schedules using lists of milestones. Whether action item tracking systems, databases that arrange milestones based on levels of priority, or documented checklists, this approach to tracking schedule never works (see Chapter 13). What invariably happens is that the owner of the action item or milestone being tracked will maintain that everything is proceeding normally and the milestone will be completed on time, until it isn't. The assertions that precede the adoption of such systems over legitimate ones usually include some sop about how *some* system was needed in the near-term, and the more appropriate systems take too long to install. Once the milestone list database is in place, its proponents will engage the economies-of-scale argument to keep in there, along the lines of "Well, it's better than nothing at all. And, now that it's in place, we don't want to come along and push a new, different system on everybody." By the time this becomes the accepted "wisdom" of the decision makers, the Greek soldiers have already poured out of the structure and are opening the main city gates.

I believe the most effective way of thwarting the Trojan horse tactic is to specifically and stridently undermine the inferior business techniques being furthered as the basis for introducing the wrong-headed practices or systems. Essentially, Cassandra's vague predictions of a tragic outcome if the real Trojan horse was wheeled past the city gates were shouted down, but she would have been more effective if she had said "It's not a gift with divine implications attached to our treatment of it. It is, in fact, a container for Greek soldiers, and if anybody were to bother to look inside, they would find I'm right about this." Now that you know the fatal flaws of the business ideas behind these managerial Trojan horses, go ahead and expose them.

Chapter Summary

The successful PMO director has the ability to quickly and accurately identify the source of the opposition to the technical agenda, and can deal with the opposition based on its source and technique. The rival systems crowd isn't confined to the elbow-aside stratagem; they are perfectly capable of launching a frontal assault. In the arena of ideas, they may attempt to use Trojan horses or code words, and, if they do, will need to be confronted with the inherent deficiencies in their approaches.

CHAPTER 15

The Damnable Need for Consensus

To me, consensus seems to be the process of abandoning all beliefs, principles, values and policies. So it is something in which no one believes and to which no one objects.

—Margaret Thatcher

The need for obtaining consensus from others in the organization in order to advance project management is a tricky proposition and much silliness has been written about it. It seemed for an interminable length of time I couldn't read *PM Network, Cost Engineering, Measurable News,* or any other trade publication without being exposed to some scold prattling on ad nauseum about the need to "engage stakeholders" in every single decision pertaining to program or project management. Although it may be obvious by now, I'll go ahead and say it: if you are waiting for all the "right" people to sign on to your efforts to implement project management within your organization, you will fail. It's inescapable. In fact, if you are pursuing your PMO implementation in such a way as to avoid making enemies at all cost, you're not doing it right, nor are you making any progress.

Ooooooo. . . . Did that last paragraph come off as harsh? Let me catch you up on your situation, PMO director:

- You have to deliver valid, timely, and accurate project management information to your organization's decision-makers.
- These decision makers are often in a position to make or break your career.
- Significant forces are arrayed against you, both overtly and covertly.
- You have a small window of opportunity to effect your tactics and achieve your goals before the organizational dynamic prevents any chance of success.
- And the obtain-approval-from-everyone crowd wants you to slow down and make everyone feel good.

Remember the reference to Bud Baker's slow roll? The seek-approval crowd is a set of ventilated disc brakes with heavy-duty calipers and synthetic brake fluid, poised and ready to slow or even stop your momentum, ruining your chances of success if they attain the smallest concession from you on how you should be pursuing your technical agenda.

A Scottish history professor Alexander Tyler wrote about the cycle of social and governmental states that all democracies would face:

- From bondage to spiritual faith,
- From spiritual faith to great courage,
- From courage to liberty,
- From liberty to abundance,
- From abundance to complacency,
- From complacency to apathy,
- From apathy to dependence, and
- From dependence back into bondage.

I submit that PMOs go through observable cycles, as well. I would further posit that those stages tend to look like this:

- Organizational acknowledgement that a PMO must be founded, usually due to some project management disaster or disasters.
- Initial enthusiasm as the PMO personnel are named, and their roles and responsibilities established.
- The energy from this initial enthusiasm is dissipated via two methods: either the PMO pursues one of the previously described tactics that don't work, or else the organization engages in slow roll or silent veto behaviors.
- The PMO attempts to tap into still more organizational power in order to overcome the bow-wave of resistance that has begun to build, usually by issuing guidance and procedures bearing the signature of the organization's top decision makers.
- When the organization still resists advancing project management techniques, the PMO resorts to a quasi-enforcement or managerial punishing agent when it perceives itself as powerful, and a whining, criticizing agent when it perceives itself to be weak. In either event, it sharply diminishes its own ability to leverage organizational power by engaging in these tactics.
- As the PMO's power to influence unravels, the hosting organization becomes complacent about its ability to successfully manage projects, programs, and portfolios using invalid information systems.
- A project management disaster occurs (which is inevitable once the organization eschews earned value and critical path). If the PMO is still in existence, its top managers are replaced. If it has ceased to exist, a new one will be created and the cycle begins again.

The funny and tragic part of this cycle lies in those managers who have been through it countless times, but lack the ability to honestly evaluate what went wrong. The reasons used to cover an unsuccessful PMO attempt almost always include vague "difficulties" in changing the macroorganization's "culture" to one that embraces project management, while the real reason sits before their very eyes: their technical approach was wrong.

It may well be that, like all democracies, all PMOs are destined to fail, and that the best possible hope for those attempting to further project management capability within their organizations is to maximize the PMO's lifespan to attain the capability maturity model's Level 4, where the level of expertise of the capability being implemented is sufficient to be exported to other organizations. At this level it is more difficult (but not impossible) for the host organization to regress, since the capability level is now a source of revenue. But achieving that level of capability requires a focused effort, pursuing the tactics that are most likely to deliver and avoiding those tactics that simply don't work.

Recall my paraphrase of Anthony Robbins from Chapter 10 that the macroorganization only changes when it is in a state of pain. The pain that led to the founding of the typical PMO is the fear of the impact of poorly executed projects leading to financial loss. This pain can be converted to energy, the power to influence decision-makers to create a project management-friendly environment where the well-executed agenda may advance. But make no mistake, this energy is finite and must be spent wisely. Pursuing tactics that don't work, making your PMO susceptible to the slow roll or silent veto or embracing the idea that universal consensus is needed before proceeding is a sure path to failure.

Successful PMOs also tend to follow a structured cycle, from my observations, and it looks like this:

- Organizational acknowledgement that a PMO must be founded, usually due to some project management disaster or disasters.
- Initial enthusiasm as the PMO personnel are named and their roles and responsibilities established.
- The new PMO director socializes EVMS reporting formats, featuring the cost and schedule performance information valued most highly by upper management.
- Using the list of criteria in Chapter 7, PMO personnel identify the work that should be managed as a project and present the bare minimum data set to be collected and the schedule for collecting it.
- With the end product established, the PMO arranges for regular meetings to evaluate all of the projects in the portfolio, with the selected EVMS report serving as the main source of performance evaluation information.
- At the performance evaluation meetings, those project teams who failed to participate in the data gathering stage, and therefore have no performance information to report, are identified. Their reasons for not participating are scrutinized and addressed, and arrangements are made for them to participate in future performance evaluation meetings.
- The PMO avoids, deflects, or overcomes the hazards listed in Part 3 of this book, and keeps the earned value information flowing.
- As the organization's decision makers begin to understand the importance of the information stream that the PMO is providing, they begin to request more or better information. At the same time, the project teams providing the *de minimus* data set become more accustomed to answering the data calls, and the EVMS begins to function more efficiently. Note that this is something of a dead-hand phenomenon—the PMO must pursue effectiveness with a single-minded fury and leave the question of higher efficiencies to be resolved later.
- The better the system gets, the more enemies the PMO makes. These will come from two sources: those parts of the organization that saw their power base shrivel as the EVMS provided superior information than they had been providing, and those poorly performing

project managers whose inferior work or shady business practices have been exposed by the EVMS. Working separately or together, these enemies will begin to damage the standing of the PMO within the organization.

- Prior to the PMO's enemies reaching critical mass, the success of the system has become so well-known (to the customers or highest-level stakeholders, with luck) that the host organization is positioned to export its capability, either directly or via proposal preparation efforts that stress an advanced capability in project management.
- Employing the three rules of implementation from Part 2 and furthering the *de minimus* EVMS package, the PMO continues to expand faster than its enemies can undermine or damage it.

Note that the end-state is dynamic, and never static. If the PMO ever ceases to add new project work to its purview, or fails to continually upgrade the accuracy, completeness, or timeliness of its information to its customers, its days are numbered. In this respect the PMO is markedly different from the typical chief financial officer organization, since the CFO's output—balance sheets and profit and loss statements—represents a static end-state. Oh, upper management might want to see the accountants' information sliced and diced in different ways—how many rented copy machines failed in comparison to the ones we bought?—but as long as the CFO organization demonstrably follows generally accepted accounting principles, there's really no threat of the organization going away. Conversely, the PMO can be among the very best at what it does, and yet remain vulnerable to it enemies, both within the organization and without.

Chapter Summary

The need for consensus feeds the slow-roll effect that can easily ruin your efforts at project management implementation. But consensus really isn't necessary, as long as the PMO has a clear-eyed view of where it is, and where it wants to go. There are essentially two paths that the PMO can take: the common one leads to a birth-death-rebirth cycle, while the one I espouse in this chapter can have a long, successful run.

Chapter 16

Conclusion

The proof of the pudding is in the eating.

—English proverb

The normal state of any organization is conflicted. In most cases there will be many mutually exclusive ideas and initiatives operating at the same time, threatening the organization's goals and objectives or even its very existence. Even in those cases where the overarching objective has been clearly articulated and openly supported, there will be many people who will work against the overall objectives in pursuit of their own agenda. When a project management practitioner is injected into such an environment, with the mission to advance the organization's project management capability, this inherent conflict can and will frustrate that mission. And when the mission to further project management is thwarted, all manner of mismanagement and the evils that accompany it will flow freely into the organization, wiping out profits, reputations, and careers.

Think I'm exaggerating? What's the first deliverable a project management practitioner will create on a new project? It's a work breakdown structure—a hierarchical listing of the decomposed project scope—essentially, the project broken down into manageable bites. Often seen as having only marginal usefulness by non-project management types, it is absolutely critical to every benefit to be had from employing project management techniques. I had the opportunity to observe what happened to a major project office that made a half-hearted attempt at developing their WBS—and it was not pretty.

The document that laid claim to being the WBS was a dog's breakfast of groups, functions, and pieces of work, blended into associations that smelled of free-form thinking to an extent that would make James Joyce proud. The schedules and cost plans that flowed from this WBS were nonsensical, clearly designed to do little more than funnel funds. Within two months, the project office was in a state of chaos, as priorities changed literally day to day. One day, the deliverables expected out of the reliability group would be in the spotlight, and their people were expected to work long hours and weekends. After barely seeing home for weeks on end, suddenly their work wasn't as important as, say, procurement. Now, rather than working overtime, the reliability analysts were suddenly in danger of being laid off, and began to seek charge codes that still had budget associated with them. In the meantime, the procurement professionals were suddenly in crisis mode, working long hours, cutting corners on procedures, desperate for help. And, just as suddenly, their danger had passed, as the focus instantly switched to the transportation group. With no structure on how the work should be planned, much less executed, the supporting groups were going between having more work than they could possibly complete within the time frames given, to being in abject fear of having no job at all. Since execution of the stated technical agenda was impossible in this environment, the manner that the employees used to gain standing in the organization turned political and nasty. Back-biting, gossip, and treachery throve, while those who were without guile suffered. What had been a nominally pleasant and professional group of people were transformed into snarling, duplicitous monsters, turning long-standing friendships into eternal animosities and laying low the dignity of any person hoping to move ahead within the confines of the project. I was young and naïve, but even then I could see what was happening, and the precise proximate cause of the project disaster. But even as I proposed to any manager who would give me a minute's time that virtually all of these problems would begin to dissipate if they would only capture the scope baseline in an adequate work breakdown structure, the occupants of the cloak room were already disparaging my reputation, slandering me clean out of the arena of ideas. It was too late for me, it was too late for them, and it was too late for the project.

Failure in the realm of project management implementation is not merely an academic or inconsequential setback. It leads to monumental wastes of time, energy, and profit. The timely completion of projects, such as the Manhattan Project, the Panama Canal, and the Patriot Missile Defense System, have literally changed lives, nations, and world history, while the timely completion of other projects, such as the coding of popular video games or the formulation of sugar substitutes, have made or ruined corporate empires, impacting millions of lives.

As you survey the organization that is expecting you to advance its project management capability, you need to be aware that fulfilling those expectations successfully is a rare thing, indeed. There are simply too many factors arrayed against you, ranging from the undying belief that organizational power can be leveraged to *make* the organization do project management, to the impacts of the vast array of the elements within the company who simply do not want you to succeed.

But success can be attained by implementing the following:

- Avoid engaging in tactics that do not work, even if those tactics are strongly supported by "leading experts" and the bulk of conventional wisdom. How do you know which tactics don't work? Read Part 1.
- Adopt the best possible technical approach, and pursue it with boatloads of energy and focus. What is the best technical approach, and why? Read Part 2.
- As you pursue the best possible technical approach, be wary of the traps and pratfalls that can bring down even the best-conceived and most energetically pursued approach. What are those traps? Read Part 3.

Now, I'm well aware that much of the project management world will criticize and reject large parts of this book, if not its entirety, if, for no other reason, than these two:

- It's not written like other management books. I'm not afraid of clearly stating my positions, unlike many other authors in this genre who appear to write as if to deflect any possible criticism.

- I'm taking on much of the conventional wisdom, especially in the realms of trainers, risk analysts, procedure writers, consultants, and software vendors. I don't anticipate that these people will stand by cheerfully as their oxen are gored.

At the end of the day, I would propose one simple test to those who disagree with the assertions in this book: did my recommendations lead to a successful PMO implementation? If they did not, you should absolutely continue to push your particular approaches and good luck to you.

But, if this book does lay out the path to successful PMO implementation, then all I have to say is: you're welcome.

References

Hatfield, M. A. 2007. PMBOK®, Schmimbock. *PM Network* 21: 1, p. 22.

Appendix A

An Earned Value Primer

Since earned value is such an integral part of advancing project management techniques, the project management office's personnel must be fluent in it. I recommend Gary Humphrey's courses (GHConsult@yahoo.com). For those who elect to read this book first, and then seek professional earned value training, this appendix will serve as a primer for earned value management systems.

What is Earned Value?

Put simply, earned value is a method for quantifying project performance. To assess the value of the work you have accomplished, multiply your percent complete by the total budget for the work. For example, if you have been offered $100 to paint a living room, and you are (verifiably) half done, you have earned $50. Note that you may not have been paid $50, nor is the $50 figure any kind of verification that you should or should not be paid that amount based on the difficulty of the work, availability of paint, etc.

The crucial thing to remember about earned value is that it is the sole method for assessing cost performance in a project.

How does it work?

Imagine that you are a project manager for a two month project, to produce 2,000 widgets, and that you have been given a $2,000 budget to do so. You time-phase your budget so that you have $1,000 in month 1, and $1,000 in month 2. At the end of month 1, your accountant comes to you and says, "You have spent $1,100 on your project."

How are you doing?

If you said "It depends on how many widgets I've made," then go to the head of the class. The knee-jerk tendency here is to assess that you have overspent, since you had budgeted $1,000, but spent $1,100, and the difference is $100. However, if you have made 1,300 widgets, then not only are you not overspent you are ahead of schedule.

There are three essential elements to earned value management systems:

1. **Time-phased budget**. This is the amount of money you planned to spend on the project, divvied up between the months of project performance. This is usually a cost estimate

based on the work breakdown structure, and spread over the period of performance. Its old moniker is the budgeted cost of work scheduled (BCWS) or just "S."

2. **Earned value figure**. This is computed in one of six ways:

   a. *Direct units.* This is what happened in the widgets story, since each widget was obviously worth $1.

   b. *Apportioned effort.* This is a companion to the direct units' method. If I plan for two gonkulators for each widget, then I would claim EV at a set ratio of gonkulators to widgets.

   c. *Milestone estimate.* Also known as the "liar's method," this is where the person responsible for the work estimates his percent complete as of the end of the reporting period. Such estimates are usually remarkably close to the percent-spent amount.

   d. *Weighted milestones.* This is a favorite. Place specifically valued milestones in the plan, and claim EV when you achieve them. A typical example is in writing a technical assessment, and the milestones are:

      i.   15% for completing the research,
      ii. 40% for completing the first draft,
      iii. 65% for completing the second draft,
      iv. 85% for shipping the document to the customer, and
      v.   100% for receiving customer approval.

   e. *Level of effort.* This is for those activities that do not have clear deliverables and milestones. The earned value figure is set equal to the amount of the time-phased budget. This method is generally discouraged.

   f. *0–100 and 50–50.* This is for short-duration activities only, and involves claiming either all or none of the budget as having been earned (0–100), or else claiming that none of it has been earned, half of it has been earned, or all of it has been earned (50–50). Earned value is also known as the budgeted cost of work performed (BCWP) or just performed (P).

3. **Actual costs**. These are generated by the organization's general ledger and represent the actual costs incurred in executing the project's goals. Actual costs are also known as the actual cost of work performed (ACWP) or actuals (A).

With these three numbers in place, you are in a position to compute an entire series of figures that will clearly indicate the project's performance, and its likely future disposition.

A cost variance, or CV, is computed:

$$\text{Cost Variance} = \text{Earned Value} - \text{Actual Costs}$$

In the widget example, we had earned $1,300 (by making 1,300 widgets at $1 each), and the actual costs were $1,100, meaning that we had a Cost Variance of a positive $200.

A schedule variance, or SV, is computed:

$$\text{Schedule Variance} = \text{Earned Value} - \text{Time-phased Budget}$$

In the widget example, we had earned $1,300, and had budgeted $1,000, producing a schedule variance of a positive $300.

The cost variance as a percentage is computed:

$$CV\% = CV / \text{Actual Costs}$$

And the schedule variance, expressed as a percentage, is:

$$SV\% = SV / \text{Time-phased budget}$$

Again, in the widget example, our cost variance as a percentage would be the $200 cost variance divided by the Actual Costs of $1,100, yielding a positive 18%. The schedule variance as a percent would be the SV of $300, divided by the budgeted amount of $1,000, yielding a whopping positive $300.

When talking variances, positive is good, negative is bad.

The cost performance index (CPI) is another performance indicator. It is used in forecast calculations, as well as a stand-alone indicator. It is computed:

$$CPI = \text{Earned Value} / \text{Actual Costs}$$

Its companion, the schedule performance index (SPI), is computed:

$$SPI = \text{Earned Value} / \text{Budget}$$

These figures are normalized around 1.00. If you CPI or SPI is over 1.00, it's good, and if it's less than 1.00, it's not so good. From the widget example, the earned value of $1,300 divided by the actual costs of $1,100 equals a CPI of 1.18. The SPI, dividing the earned value of $1,300 by the budget of $1,000, yields an SPI of 1.3. Note that in each of these calculations, you always start with the earned value figure. Also note that there are no calculations that directly compare the budgets to the actual costs.

As mentioned in the book, a common method of calculating the forecast costs at project completion, known as the Estimate at Completion, or EAC, is:

$$EAC = \text{Total Budget} / CPI$$

Since any number divided by 1 is that number, you can see why a CPI of over 1.00 is a good thing. It means that your EAC will be less than the budget. Conversely, if your CPI is less than 1.00, then the EAC will be greater than the budget, indicating a potential overrun. From the widget example, the total budget of $2,000, divided by the CPI of 1.18, means that, at this rate of performance, the widget project will be completed at a total cost of $1,695.

A variance at completion is the difference between the EAC and the total budget. This figure often presages total profit or total loss, and will often attract a good deal of attention. Since the widget project had a total budget of $2,000, and it will probably be completed for $1,695, it stands to make a profit of $305, or over 15%. Not a bad rate of return, eh, accountants?

There are a variety of formats that can be used to show this information, from the complex to the highly intuitive. In the early stages of the PMO, always opt for the more intuitive—at least until you can get to an EVMS class.